frank: sonnets

Also by Diane Seuss

Still Life with Two Dead Peacocks and a Girl
Four-Legged Girl
Wolf Lake, White Gown Blown Open
It Blows You Hollow

frank: sonnets

Diane Seuss

Graywolf Press

This publication is made possible, in part, by the voters of Minnesota through a Minnesota State Arts Board Operating Support grant, thanks to a legislative appropriation from the arts and cultural heritage fund. Significant support has also been provided by Target Foundation, the McKnight Foundation, the Lannan Foundation, the Amazon Literary Partnership, and other generous contributions from foundations, corporations, and individuals. To these organizations and individuals we offer our heartfelt thanks.

Published by Graywolf Press
212 Third Avenue North, Suite 485
Minneapolis, Minnesota 55401

www.graywolfpress.org

Published in the United States of America

ISBN 978-1-64445-045-1

6 8 10 12 13 11 9 7 5

Library of Congress Control Number: 2020937626

Cover design: Jeenee Lee

Cover photo: Alan Martinez, *Mikel Lindzy*

To—you know—*you*.

And for my sister.

Contents

"This is my barbed wire dress. It protects the property but doesn't hide the view."
—*Candy Darling*

"Feel like a lady, and you my lady boy."—*Amy Winehouse*

"Frank has asked me to announce that none of the sentiments expressed in this poem are his. They're mine."—*Elaine de Kooning*

frank: sonnets

I drove all the way to Cape Disappointment but didn't

have the energy to get out of the car. Rental. Blue Ford

Focus. I had to stop in a semi-public place to pee

on the ground. Just squatted there on the roadside.

I don't know what's up with my bladder. I pee and then

I have to pee and pee again. Instead of sightseeing

I climbed into the back seat of the car and took a nap.

I'm a little like Frank O'Hara without the handsome

nose and penis and the New York School and Larry

Rivers. Paid for a day pass at Cape Disappointment

thinking hard about that long drop from the lighthouse

to the sea. Thought about going into the Ocean

Medical Center for a checkup but how do I explain

this restless search for beauty or relief?

The problem with sweetness is death. The problem

with everything is death. There really is no other problem

if you factor everything down, which I was no good at

when studying fractions. They were always using pie

as their example. Rather than thinking about factoring

things down, I wondered what kind of pie. And here

I am, broke, barely able to count to fourteen. When

people talk about math, they say you'll need it to balance

your checkbook. What is a checkbook and what,

indeed, is balance? Speaking of sweetness, for a time

I worked in a fudge shop on an island. After a week

the smell of sweetness made me heave, not to mention

the smell of horses; it was an island without cars,

shit everywhere. When I quit, the owner slapped me.

Intimacy unhinged, unpaddocked me. I didn't want it.

Believe me, I didn't want it anymore. Who in their

right mind? And then it came like an ice cream truck

with its weird tinkling music, its sweet frost. I fled

to the shore and saw how death-strewn, all the body

parts washed up and sucked clean like that floor mosaic

by Sosus of Pergamon, *Unswept House.* Seabirds

flocked and dematerialized like they do. Bees raged

at their own dethroning. Love came close anyway,

found me out, its warped music all the rage. It had

a way, just by being in proximity, of opening

the shells of the bivalves. Disclosing their secret

meat. One doesn't really *suck* on frozen sugar water.

One allows it to melt in the oven of the mouth.

I met a man a dying man and I said me too.
Met a dead man and I said me too. Must be
dead cuz the living can't meet the dead and he
said me too. Did you know the dead can fall
in love he said. Fact. Did you know the dead
fall in love better than the living cuz nothing
left to lose. The root of all blues. Skeptical still
I strode onward in my seven-league boots as in
the fairy tale "Hop-o'-My-Thumb" from a book
of German fairy tales given to me when I had
chicken pox. Scratching myself bloody, the ogre
gored to death by wild beasts. Seven leagues per
stride toward a dead banjo player in a bad
mood. *Enchanteur.* Or *zauberhaft* in German.

It is abominable, unquenchable by touch, closer

to the sublime than sentimental, more animal

than hominid, I've seen it in the eyes of birds

weaving on a stem of ragweed, voracious,

singular, there is no one like me, Dickinson in

her narrow bed, her cold clenched hands, her

penmanship unreadable, even following a recipe

for black cake, her black cake came out strange,

lusher than the template, and every freak I ever

met had that same look in their eyes, armless,

threading a needle with their lips and teeth,

legless, rounding a corner on their cerulean cart,

monarchic, imperious, wild, sad, and like every

virgin queen, the need for love revolting and grand.

Sometimes I can't feel it, what some call

beauty. I can see it, I swear, the conifers

and fat bees, ferns like church fans and then

the sea, its flatness as if pressed by stones

like witches were, the dark sand ridged

by tides, strewn with body parts, claws,

the stranded mesoglea of the moon jellyfish,

transparent blob, brainless, enlightened in its clarity.

I stand there, I walk the shore at low tide, the sky

fearless, not open to me, just open, there it is,

the wind, cold, surf's boom drowning out

thought, I can photograph it, I can name it

beautiful, but feel it, I don't know that I am

feeling it, when I drown in it, maybe then.

I could do it. I could walk into the sea.

I have a rental car. It's blue and low on fuel.

I have feet, two, and proximity. I could do it.

Others have before me. Jeff Buckley (1997) he

was only 30. Carol Wayne (1985) the Matinee Lady

and a photo spread in *Playboy*. Dennis Wilson (1983)

after diving for a photo of his ex-wife he'd tossed

overboard years earlier. Hart Crane, well of course

Hart Crane (1932). Socialite Starr Faithfull (1931),

she was only 25, she drowned in shallow water near

the shore, her lungs all full of sand. Starr left behind

her sex diary, current whereabouts unknown. 19 men.

It's dark. I love the dark and it loves me.

It would be fun! I could walk into the sea!

Press a foot into this beach and blood

will ooze up instead of saltwater. If there

are poems, let them come in sick waves

like pushing contractions for a birth I did

not have the strength to finish. Cut me, cut me!

They cut me stem to stern and out came a little

drug addict. Do you know the houses here are built

from shipwrecks? That the nondenominationals

host a vespers service in a chapel whose weekly

whitewashing will not staunch the bleeding

of the wood? The mad reversals: fawns are carnivores,

coyotes whine for edible flowers. Each morning

glory a tsunami siren. Cut me! The ocean too

is red though it thought it was exempt.

The best is when you respond only to the absolute present

tense, the rain, the rain, rain, rain, and wind, an iridescent

cloud, another shooting, this time in a shopping mall

in Germany, so this is why people want other people to put

their arms around them, I will walk to the bay where there is

a kind of peace, even emptiness, the barn swallows' sharp

flight and cry, who now has the luxury of emptiness or peace,

the beauty of thunder in a place where there is rarely thunder,

the mind like a jackrabbit bounding, bounding, my wet hair

against my neck, grandfather's barber shop, the lineup

of hair tonics by color like a spectrum, the pool table removed

to make a room for great grandma to live out her years, my

father cutting a semicircle in her kitchen table so it would fit

around the stovepipe, rain, rain, fascism in America is loud.

From this bench I like to call my bench I sit

and watch my tree which is not my tree, no one's

tree, the quiet! Except for barn swallows which are

not loud birds, how many exclamation points can I

get away with in this life, who was it who said only two

or maybe seven, Bishop? Marianne Moore? Either way

the world is capable of quiet if everyone stays indoors

and no jet planes, my tree, it just stands there

in the middle of everything in a meadow on the bay

looking what Barthes called "adorable," then I drove

the mile west to the sea which had decided to be loud

that day, the sunset, oh, ragged and bloody as a piece

of raw meat in the jaws of some big golden carnivore,

and I cried a little, for none of it! none of it will last!

Poetry, the only father, landscape, moon, food, the bowl

of clam chowder in Nahcotta, was I happy, mountains

of oyster shells gleaming silver, poetry, the only gold,

or is it, my breasts, feet, my hands, index finger,

fingernail, hangnail, paper cut, what is divine, I drove

to the sea, wandered aimlessly, I stared at my tree, I said

in my mind *there's my tree*, there's my tree I said in my mind,

I remember myself before words, thrilled at my parents'

touch, opened milkweed with no agenda, blew the fluff,

no reaching for comparison, to be free of signification,

wriggle out of the figurative itchy sweater, body, breasts,

vulva, little cave of the uterus, clit, need, touch, come, I came

before I knew what coming was, iambic pentameter, did I

feel it, does language eclipse feeling, does it eclipse the eclipse.

Here on this edge I have had many diminutive visions. That all at its essence is dove-gray.

Wipe the lipstick off the mouth of anything and there you will find dove-gray. With my

thumb I have smudged away the sky's blue and the water's blue and found, when I kicked it

with my shoe, even the sand at its essence is pelican-gray. I am remembering Eden.

How everything swaggered with color. How the hollyhocks finished each other's sentences.

How I missed predatory animals and worrying about being eaten. How I missed being eaten.

How the ocean and the continent are essentially love on a terrible mission to meet up with itself.

How even with the surface roiling, the depths are calmly nursing away at love. That look the late

nurser gets in its eyes as it sucks: a habitual, complacent peace. How to mother that peace, to wean

it, is a terrible career. And to smudge beauty is to discover ugliness. And to smudge ugliness is to be

knocked back by splendor. How every apple is the poison apple. How rosy the skin. How sweet

the flesh. How to suck the apple's poison is the one true meal, the invocation and the Last

Supper. How stillness nests at the base of wind's spine. How even gravestones buckle and swell

with the tides. And coffins are little wayward ships making their way toward love's other shore.

To return from Paradise I guess they call that

resurrection. Don't remember the black cherries'

gleam, bay shine, mountain's sheen, blissful

appalling loneliness. Messy foam at sea's edge,

slurry they call it, where love and death meld

into slop and unaccustomed birds. Forget all

the way back to where you were before you were

born. When Dyl was a toddler, still finger-sucking,

he said he remembered the sound of my blood

whooshing past him in utero, maybe the first of many

lies, this one with an adorable speech impediment.

I always return, it's my nature, like the man who

couldn't stop liberating the crayfish even though

it pinched him hard, *that* song, *that* grand ole opry.

What is it you feel, I asked Kurt when you listen to

Ravel's String Quartet in F Major, his face was so lit up

and I wondered, "the music is unlike the world I live

or think in, it's from somewhere else, unfamiliar and unknown,

not because it is relevant to the familiar and comfortable,

but because it brings me to that place that I didn't/couldn't

imagine existed. And sometimes that unfamiliar place is closer

to my world than I realize, and sometimes it's endlessly distant,"

that's what he wrote in an email when I asked him

to remind me what he'd said earlier, off the cuff, "I don't

recall exactly what I said," he began, a sentence written

in iambic pentameter, and then the rest, later he spoke of two

of his brothers who died as children, leukemia and fire,

his face, soft, I'm listening to Ravel now, its irrelevancy.

Listening to "Summertime" played by Kurt Rohde on

viola, when did my heart break, at birth, all of our little

hearts like little acorns break. You must go to it,

whatever it is, like a flayed dog it will not come to you,

for I am like Tony, a provocateur at heart, and he has a tumor

in his pancreas so where did all the provocation get him,

Pam would say it's not your job to rip the Band-Aid

from someone else's wound and clearly she is right,

why say or do anything, I suppose "I love you" will suffice

but now and then, the Band-Aid's little upturned corner

beckons like dead Ahab lashed to the whale's side, something

presses to be said or read, listened to or forgotten, a tune

that opens your flesh, removes the bones, fillets you till you die,

the jumping fish, the rich daddy, the hush baby don't you cry.

There is a certain state of grace that is not loving.

Music, Kurt says, is not a language, though people

say it is. Even poetry, though built from words,

is not a language, the words are the lacy gown,

the something else is the bride who can't be factored

down even to her flesh and bones. I wore my own

white dress, my hair a certain way, and looked into

the mirror to get my smile right and then into my own

eyes, it's rare to really look, and saw I was making

a fatal mistake, that's the poem, but went through

with it anyway, that's the music, spent years in

a graceful detachment, now silence is my lover, it does

not embrace me when I wake, or it does, but its embrace

is neutral, like God, or Switzerland since 1815.

"No need to sparkle," Virginia Woolf wrote in *A Room*

of One's Own, oh, would that it were true, I loved the kids

who didn't, June, can't remember her last name, tilt of her

head like an off-brand flower on the wane, her little rotten

teeth the color of pencil lead, housedresses even in 4th grade,

and that boy Danny Davis, gray house, horse, eyes, clothes,

fingertips and prints, freckles not copper-colored but like metal

shavings you could clean up with a magnet. Now Mrs. LaPointe

was a dug-up bone but Miss Edge sparkled, taught the half-

and-half class, 3rd and 4th grades cut down the middle

of the room like sheet cake, wore a lavender chiffon dress

with a gauzy cape to school, aquamarine eye shadow, "Sweetie,"

she whispered to me, leaning down, breath a perfume, "your

daddy's dead," tears stuck to her cheeks like leeches or jewels.

My earliest memory is telling myself stories without

words, starring the decal dog, cat, and butterfly

on my crib headboard, I couldn't talk yet, then my

mother coming in the room to pick me up, I lifted

my arms, it must have been my mother though I've

never called her mother in my life, I call her by her

name, Norma, and always have, another early memory

is getting lost in a toy store, finding my mother

and encircling her legs with my arms, but it was not my

mother, it was another lady, a stranger, and from then on

toys too were strange, the small oven that baked cakes

with a light bulb, playing under a mock orange tree

and in the abandoned chicken coop, finding out

what I called violets was really petrified chicken shit.

Since age three, I went looking for salvation, the village was safe

it was believed, and the churches within toddling distance, so

I toddled to the Methodists, Presbyterians, Baptists, and to the best

and worst of all, the Church of God between the cemetery

and rhubarb patch, cement blocks painted white and a misspelled

sign, Bible school was severe, required memorization, much religion

seems to require memorization by children, I won a two-inch plastic

manger scene with glitter on the roof for my recitation of John 3:16,

there's your sins, teacher sneered, after making us put red polka dots

all over the hearts we'd cut with safety scissors from white paper,

now go get saved, and I did, seven times, I even went to catechism,

but the brother said I was too young to convert, he wore thick

glasses, his face covered in acne scars, the best part of getting saved

was diving into the old pastor's big belly, I could see his undershirt.

Who wants to be soft? I don't. I've even seen a hermit crab

outgrow its shell and drag its perilous softness into a doll's head.

Crab, I empathize. As a kid, I fed my big baby doll's bare foot

into a rotating fan blade. I wasn't mean, not at all. Inquisitive.

Doll donated her toe to science. I mixed potions: iodine, nightshade,

and some incongruity like a few drops of my dad's aftershave. He was

dead by then, but there was a quarter of a bottle of Aqua Velva

in the medicine chest, which I used sparingly. I wasn't planning to poison

anyone, even my sister, who showed me how to harden up by folding

her arms across her chest and scowling at dad's abdominal tumor.

Our mom slammed the door and drove to Lake Michigan. I pictured her

making her way into the sheltering undertow. The Rev. Larry Whiteford

sang "When the Gates Swing Open" at the funeral, and the three of us

sat there like Mt. Rushmore. Anyway, dad was a softie, Jesus, a softie.

I was raised in a rectangle. Aluminum. There was a rectangular

toy box, red. Sometimes, I'd take out the toys and climb inside.

Rectangle within a rectangle. In my mind, I'd sing a song called

"My Tiny Childhood." Sometimes, I'd let a doll stay. I liked to sit

in the pile of dirty laundry that had overflowed the clothes hamper.

A yeasty, mortal smell. I smelled that way in England after a grueling

journey over the English Channel on a ferry from Hoek van Holland

to Harwich. An East German man with a red face, he could not hear

nor speak but gestured wildly for another drink. A British soldier

with scented pomade in his hair. Two Scottish soldiers, twins, kilts,

one of whom wrote my mother a postcard asking for my hand.

By the time she got it, I was long gone, had climbed many stairs

to a blue rectangle in London, clock tower bell bonging outside

the window, slept for hours unburdened by conscience, like a baby.

I was not a large child, though large in silence, learned

from pods and brambles and cattail's velvet fruit. Like

the world, which began as a pea-sized notion under

the mattress of an oversensitive girl, I grew vast, too vast,

it was said, for my landscape's monsters: cows, mudpuppies,

bullfrogs, Polyphemus moths with purple eyespots on their wings,

nightcrawlers in the worm bin, catalpas inside out on the hook,

nature, outmoded as stockings with a seam up the back, as rations

and iron pills and traction for back pain, dad strung up

and weighed down until they figured out it was a tumor. I flew

far away to feel molecular, but even among the throng, my life

was enormous, a raucous tragedy, having outgrown its theater's

cherubs and filmy purple curtains and thereby gushing

out into the street, filling it with arterial soliloquys.

Freak accidents do happen, girl said it ten, twelve times that night,

her pronouncement curled in my head for decades, a tequila worm,

my sister and I snowbound in a cold house, our mother stranded somewhere,

sleeping, she said, in a public library, I pictured her under a blanket

of paperbacks, power out so we tracked each other's breath

in the flashlight beam, that girl, somebody from the neighborhood,

made it through the snow to play a role in our tragedy, maybe snowshoed,

wouldn't put it past her, freak accidents, she said, moving the candle

to the center of the table because fire turns little girls to cinders, I was eight,

my sister twelve, blizzard brought out her kinder nature, normally she'd

have used this as a chance to murder me, we ate saltines and margarine

huddled in bed, don't choke, the freak-girl said, wind whining, power lines

writhing and crackling across 13th St., our father shivering in his coffin

under all that snow, oh, that freckled oracle, Lizzy Ferris was her name.

My first crush was Wild Bill Hickok, not the actual guy but the guy who portrayed him

on TV, Guy Madison, who died of emphysema, whose grandson was killed in action in Iraq.

What did cowboys do all day, I wondered. Aside from gunfighting. Figuring out whether

they'd be good or bad, which determined the color of the hat. My hat, how did my mother

afford it, bought at West's Variety, powder blue. My gun, a toy. I was wise enough at age

three to own my projections. I would become what I loved. My mother didn't hover

as I decided what I'd do with what I was. Her best friend made a particle board lid for the crib

so she could go out on the cement slab and drink highballs, unimpeded by kids, who all

turned out fine and loved her madly, though half of them died young in motorcycle wrecks.

My mother didn't care if I rescued or killed or swung from a noose until I was dead. That

was my domain. Her domain was TV dinners and James Joyce. Mikel's first crush was the body

of a young hung TV cowboy who swung from the noose in a spiral pattern. Mikel called home

his projections and likewise died young and hung. I decided my kind of cowboy would read

tall tales from a tall book called *Tall Tales* about tornadoes and card games and white whales.

They lived next door, four boys, meek dad, and Mary Lou, their mom, who had good reason

to be unhinged and she was unhinged, the oldest boy they had on a leash tied to a clothesline

like a dog, the youngest would sit on the corner eating cracker sandwiches, a four-square

of saltines between two slices of white bread spread with yellow mustard, who one night

got into Mary Lou's diet pills and made strange markings all over the bathtub with black

crayon and climbed to the top of the curio cabinet like a squirrel, then one of the middle

boys, peanut-headed, rolled over my pet caterpillar with his bike wheel so sluggishly

the guts oozed in slow motion, and let's just say I'd suffered for that caterpillar, nailed

holes in the lid of its jar and studied up on its diet, it was Pat or Tom, peanut-headed

either way, I knocked him off his bike and sat on his stomach and stuffed grass in his

mouth, and next door to them, a woman lived alone in a low white house, it was said she

had a sunken living room and white shag carpeting, a taxidermized tiger and an uncaged

parrot who flew through the rooms and spoke in tongues, but I don't know, I never was

inside, the only one who wormed her way in was Mary Lou and her testimony was unreliable.

I suck so many cough drops that my pee is mentholated. Not for pleasure.

For pain. I cough. It hurts. Though as a kid if given the choice of candies

I'd pick Vicks lozenges. From there it was boys clothes. Wore a pack

of candy cigarettes in the T-shirt pocket. Vicks in the pocket of my jeans.

Had access to matches from the bowling alley. Charred the cigarette end, once

set the whole pack on fire. Yes, I played with matches. No one knew or cared.

That was my luck. I learned early to swallow pills so I could take knockoff

One A Day vitamins we got free from my mom's friend who worked in the pill factory.

I'd suck off the sweet coating before swallowing the iron that made my little turds

black. I was glad my dad was sick. It gave me access to him. I could sit next to him

and hold his cold bones in my hands. Trace the blue veins and the incision

that wrapped his torso like a feather boa or a boa constrictor. I was a quiet child

but I schemed behind the silence. Already setting up the terms of my survival

like chess pieces whose royalty I coveted. Black army on a stolen board.

I floated I flew I fell to Earth to learn the pleasures of the lowdown

which meant sometimes going downtown to the Ready theater

to get my ticket punched by ole hook-for-a-hand I feared ambulances

janitors knives dogwood blossoms my sister's boyfriends one of whom

threw a knife at my head one of whom pressed his whiskers into my face

and whispered things my girlfriends' boyfriends one of whom shot me

in the bone behind my ear at a shooting gallery my unspayed dog's periods

we put her in my sister's bikini underpants stuffed with a Kotex pad the girl

whose eyes were crossed cowboy boots on the wrong feet the birthmark

girl Dwight who saw through me Little S hit and killed by a jeep on 13th St.

the guy who hit him sticking his tongue in my mouth at an adult party

Jesus the eschaton which I learned from a well-read Jehovah's Witness

was a synonym for the end of the world my father resurrecting

my father not resurrecting I feared floating flying falling the lowdown.

That bar, World of the Satisfyin' Place, cream-colored sign with bullet holes. Bullet holes

in the back end of Villeneuve's gold Lincoln, he was still getting residuals from his stint

as the keyboardist for the Shondells, died young of Hep C, that was a cold blow. I fed him

pickles from a jar in his car and bled on the seat. State Line Supermarket burned. I sat

on an upended crate and ate pickles hot from the fire with the owner's daughter. She was giddy

as people get when their lives go up in smoke. Her big eyes gleamed like they did when she

played Maria in *The Sound of Music*. I was Gretl, a thrill, though knocked unconscious by Friedrich

during the thunderstorm scene. Drive-in movie screen burned, I stood and watched, sleeveless

undershirt, hands on my hips. Tragic spectacle my realm, I its ruthless queen. Elvis died hard

that day, burned alive on a Ferris wheel with a smile on his face. My first thrill at the hands

of another was when Twin sat on the small of my back and gave me a back rub. This was before

the white Jesus kids got to her. Made her quit dancing, eating cheeseburgers. Snapped her glasses

in half and said if God wanted her to see he'd heal her eyes. Her hands were strong. Fingers

long. I didn't have a word for that baroque pleasure, but I knew better than to thank her.

Labels now slip off me like clothes when I was in the dark

with some daddy-man and I could turn anyone into a daddy-man

with my stupendous mind which is how I thought about things

when I was fourteen and some half-a-rapist was scraping the tears

off my cheeks with a milkweed pod in his two-room house

on the riverbank so many boys back home lived without parents

in Fuckerson Park where some of us teetered ready to tip onto dirt

roads where shacks were painted Kool-Aid colors and nameless

pathways led to Bob's Country Club and all the dogs were named

Pee Hole and one big colonial prefab from when the Lord led Rose

to the right lottery ticket which wasn't worth the resentment heaped

on her by the rest of us even Jesus she said resented her and smote her

that way he does with a thousand paper cuts which made the rest of us feel

better and that is the job of Jesus the most daddyish daddy-man of all.

All at once David went catatonic, you could pose him and he'd freeze

that way, then Steve showed up skinned alive from flying off his motorcycle

on US 31 as it was called then, all to deliver to me a comb for my hair

he found when he was working on a barge on the Mississippi, he smiled

through the blood on his face, laughed like a sandhill crane at the luck

of his misfortune, we'd had some good times hitching to Eau Claire for ice

cream, a small cone is all, he played the harmonica and I hummed, the road

hot and flat, rippling with the mirage of water, but good times do not a love

story make, though I peeled off what was left of his clothes and sacrificed

a full bottle of hydrogen peroxide to the singular wound that was his body

and dressed him in a ratty shirt and pants which had served me well as a hobo

costume though the green hat had melted in the rain, and fed him watery soup

from a can, and sent him home on a train though I did not pay, I didn't have

money in those days, nor did I love God, nor David even when he thawed.

I want drugs again; whimsy. Frenzy, hilarity, as when

visiting mass with Juanita, we were twelve, I wasn't

Catholic, laughing ourselves sick at the names of saints,

Linus, Cletus, Clement, Sixtus, sparks went off in my

brain, I had no squeamishness, I'd eat alligator, rabbit

with the head on, fish eggs, eyes, hitchhike playing

the mouth harp, got into a helluva jam, sitting in the cab

of a truck between two nasty bumpkins, saved when

a turkey vulture crashed through the windshield into

my lap, Jesus was looking out for me that day, celebrated

not being murdered at a bar that rose out of the fog

like an iceberg, I was wearing a stolen blue smoking

jacket I called a kimono, yes I was a knave, a fool,

Cornelius, Cyprian, Chrysogonus, Cosmas, and Damian.

His body was barely cold when the suitors swooped in on the young widow, the ground was still fresh over the grave, it was spring, the president had been shot a few months earlier, nests mocked the gravedigger's work, the suitors swooped in from all directions like carrion birds, the first an oval-headed man from across the road with dirty phone calls the night after the funeral, then one cornered her in the garage by the bag of her husband's clothes, and two brothers peeked in the windows and tapped on them like woodpeckers, and the school ring salesman, and the old man who looked like Colonel Sanders, and Al, her friend's husband from Wabash, Indiana, while his wife was strapped down getting shock treatments, and the small man with a big voice who pawed in the night at the screen door like a bear roaring her name, just a few months earlier she'd watched the president's funeral on television, there was Black Jack, riderless horse, boots set backward in the stirrups, and the president's widow, walking straight-spined under a black veil, and now the robins hopped as they always had, their songs like a tangle of string in the air, and how did she fend them off, the suitors, and go to college, and read *Ulysses*, and write papers on that manual typewriter, and feed us, my sister and me?

The lambs this year are dumb but lambs are dumb

their tiny brains archaic smiles humans to a lamb

are all the same all rams the same all ewes are mom

all milk is mine all lambs are me all blades of grass

a single blade of grass incapable of love unlike a pig

who aims to please who specifies who trots behind

as loyal as a dog and kisses like a dog its tongue

astonishingly soft who grieves when led away when

loaded up when walked into the marketplace who'd

die of grief if held too long to get to slaughter

weight nostalgic for the hills the mist the girl the battered

truck she pedaled to the barn the chickens who have no

self at all who yearn as one who peck the flat terrain

as one who rise as one and fall as one like rain.

One's got an eye thing that makes her walk on her tiptoes

one's got a brain thing that gives him the quivers another's

got a brain thing that falls him down a brain thing that rises

him one won't leave the house another won't come home one's

got a goat that strips leaves off the grapevines one butchered

a hog the kids slept on like a pillow one glories in the Lord

and it gives her bad conniptions one glories and caterwauls

one's deaf to caterwauling one's stuck on the memory of wild

lupines one thinks back on the showy flowers of the male

goatsbeard the root beer scent of sassafras one stands on a cable

spool and orates fairy tales to stunted inbred lambs one's got

a brain thing puts a wrench in her remembering one with an eye

thing puts a crick in his forgetting one recalls when the earthstars

went away whose fungal petals shivered and opened in the rain.

When the lamb humped her leg Lil said it was getting on

her last nerve and she declined to show it at the fair

so Ell was stuck with it Ell was built as they say like a brick

shithouse resentful dutiful long-suffering preferring the pigs

who actually feel who care maybe even love Lil was the type

who carried a rabbit around in her purse black rabbit red purse

the rabbit seemed happy enough the house covered in the pollen

of Cheetos dust and what Lil called her projects milkweed pods

painted into pink ships the fluff airborne in the current from

the window fan Ell her hair slicked off her forehead a tight ponytail

cowboy shirt tucked into her jeans it matters in this business how

you look not just the performance of the animal she thought

but never spoke her thoughts and tried to have as few thoughts

as possible if you want the grand prize you must keep a quiet mind.

After the pigs and lambs and rabbits were sold off at auction they

bought a 30-dollar goat and named it Snowflake Brownie and then

a second one called Cookie Dough the third Brandon but the names

melded they were dubbed the Healing Goats brought to the farm to keep

the girls from being so busted up over Pork Chop Charlotte Cotton Candy

Sophie Zoey and Chloe raising them up only to sell them off for slaughter

it's a mistake to name them but kids name even rocks when I was young

I named a stone Burnt Umber and kept it in a ring box in my pocket symbolic

of the horse I would never have the younger girl allowed herself to be consoled

by the goats' horizontal pupils their swift heartbeats and she grew from there

into a full-blown sentimentalist while the older girl kept the goats at arm's length

averse to being charmed out of her grief which was really anger at God

unable it turns out to once again love but it was she who became a well-to-do

farmer a devoted cynic her mouth drawn into a tight line like a lead rope.

The parents tried to build a little Eden aboveground pool cigar box
full of crayons 24-hour access to junk food and the kids could eat
anytime anywhere and not clean up after themselves soggy
Tupperware bowls of sugar cereal on the end tables Little Debbie
filling smeared on the couch what the hell life is short new animals
to replace the ones sold off or dead barn cats everywhere until all
the inbred kittens were born blind the goats got lungworms
and the ones who stayed healthy leaped the fence and ran away
the uncontainable dog got smashed by an ice cream truck on Born St.
the trampoline was impaled on a tree during a tornado the produce
that was to be sold on the honor system at the roadside stand did not
come to fruition and the money from what they managed to harvest
was stolen by the mailman's kids so it turned out it was all for naught
the kids learned more about death than life just like the rest of us.

The fat suffering of the farrowing sow. Salty-sweet of blood and hay

like a carnival. The girls learn from the pig born blue. Lil cries, Ell says

it happens, mom. Brian's out on the train. He keeps watch for suicides

on the tracks. -40 wind chills. Lil holds a live one under her coat, pig's

gray cord hanging out at the hem. Blood freezes on her pajamas. Momma

suffers to rid herself of each fancy body. Pigs have more hair than you'd

think. Ice-white, and long white lashes. Eight altogether if you count the dead

one, and one is crushed when Momma rolls over on it in her sleep. The biggest

they name Moose. There's a runt that goes nameless, doesn't give a shit,

finds its way to tit and more tit. The sow loves none of them, moons only

over the woman who tends her, won't eat until she comes to the barn.

The fate of the living children: sold off, kept as pets, grown into slaughter,

mothers themselves. Some wander and walk along the tracks in the rain

like Judy the singing minister's daughter who stepped in front of a train.

The patriarch of Jesus Camp is dead! Father of Greg who dragged a giant cross across the high school parking lot on Good Friday is dead! Father of Charity who wore pink housedresses to high school is dead! White anklets. Orthopedic shoes. Duck-faced Charity who Jesus stole early. Embezzled. Hijacked to heaven before we were ready. It's not fair we cried! Ground our teeth in our sleep. Had to get bite splints. Even if the streets are paved with gold we said. Even if Charity can chip off some gold and use it to buy cosmetics. As if Heaven has a Hook's drugstore. As if being pretty counts in a place where everything is pretty. The patriarch only smiled. That way he did with a weed sticking out of the corner of his mouth. Charity was his daughter but he said and I quote "To be absent from the body is to be present with the Lord!" What does that look like exactly we cried. Are there chairs? Are there lambs to tend? Because you know how we get when there are no lambs to tend! He had a look in his eye like Charity had given him previews of coming attractions. But his lips were sealed and now they're sealed for good and now only an echo from the grotto.

It was a land without charm without debauchery nothing witnessed nothing made no visions divisions no Burger Chef there was no B & L with the metal cow on the roof no meat patties no Smokey Joe no briquettes no Kmart there was no Kmart submarine sandwiches no blue light specials carts bursting with merchandise there was no tank in the parking lot with Flipper visiting from Florida no names of states no state lines there was no Houdini Jr. no box dropped from the bridge into the river holding Houdini Jr. wrapped in padlocked chains there was no jukebox there was no Al Green Sam no Tammy there was no soul no deep-fried whities no house trailer there was no beguiling no subdivision no furrow no factory no beauty carnivorous plants there was pitchers sundews labial inflorescences purple nodding on their stems in the boglands.

The White Rabbit was before the high-rise, bras stuffed with socks, you can

hear it in the breeze, boys wanted boobs. Cattails hammered the wind.

Mr. K's too fancy. Remember Satan's Inn. 'Bout beat a bitch's ass on the pool

table, glass floor lit up red back then. Mansion changed into a hospital, gazebo

across from the Catholics. Remember Joe Savage and his Snake Act, Mrs. Funk.

Remember the whorehouse by the depot back when it still had a ticket window.

Nobody cared their teeth were small and green. Where was Pecker's Pond,

where was Penis Rock. Who remembers the mustache Betty wore to the men's

side of the wire factory. Shondell who died mysterious. Remember cancer

clusters on Pucker Rd., something wrong with the wells, dumped cyanide in a pit

and built over it. Brown cloud. When Bill dove and broke his neck people

thought he was playing drowned. Who shimmied, soul kissed. French inhaled,

jerked. River drank Wonderland and the button factory. Since the flooding,

everything's a blur. Was was all there was and was was what we were.

They wander in, two Southdowns, those lambs that always smile,

black lambs that smile but not from happiness, they wander in,

twin lambs we christen Jack and Jill whose fleece resembles

smoke trees in the rain, whose hopeless bleats for mama bring us

hope but not the hopeful kind, their pupils coffin-lid horizon lines,

their lashes human, stark and white like lashes of the blind, they cogitate,

they meditate their food, they muse it through their many-chambered

selves, then Jill rebels and climbs the hill where apple trees and rock

elms grow, and Jack, a follower, he follows her, up the fabled nameless

hill to the brook that burbles up from Purgatory, it's this spring the twin

lambs seek, and yes it's green and yes it's sweet, without the tinny aftertaste

of pail, and so they wander off the trail, abandoning their bedding straw

enlaced with lavender, their straps and copper bells, across the mead

they stride and never down, forsaking their sweet apple-blossom crowns.

He came to us all the way down here with us he trod the narrow

path to us he harrowed us he robbed us of our stuff and then he

bade us to adore the very robber who had robbed us of ourselves

he swept his empty hand across our shelves he commandeered

our dust he loosed the goats rejoined the milky mothers to their

calves he cut our drooping fruits in halves infringed upon our lust

he mesmerized the feral cats and charmed them from the pee-marked

corners of the barn into god-awful light he strode across our ashes

and our blight the fields we'd burned to rid ourselves of parasitic

worms and ticks he snared our seeds and jarred our feeble bees

he gathered up our kids the ones who squeezed their dirty feet into

ill-begotten shoes the brood of meth and Thunderbird whose amniotic

sacs were tinted blue he harrowed us unbarrowed us he sparrowed us

and nailed us then he jacked our 7-Eleven and he hauled us up to heaven.

For a couple years, I slept nights in Babe's basement on a low gold couch right up

next to the wood burner, mom had been displaced from her own house, long story,

so my sister and her kids and husband could live there, they'd crossed the bridge

to move back home because Em had a hole between two chambers of her heart,

mom stayed in a one-room place, a little crouching house set back off the road

behind the trailer park, kerosene lamp, nowhere for me to sleep, so I'd run across

the yard and crawl under the barbed wire to Babe's basement door, they'd keep it

unlocked for me, when I needed to pee, I slipped out the door in the middle

of the night to unbridle my stream like an animal, squat and watch the snow steam,

and back inside where the fire logs too were animals, settling in and licking each other

with blue tongues, Vic was still alive then, Vic Sr., he had his shop set up down

there for rock polishing, agates and tiger eyes, pick, he said once, and I chose a fire

opal, I guess the conditions of our lives were bad but I was at peace, feeding logs into

the stove's mouth, alone with the precious stones, there in the fabled underground.

Once, I took a Greyhound north across an icy bridge, it seemed it took

all night to cross that bridge, a bridge lined with stars unscrewed

from the sky and fastened to the cables and the towers with black

electrical tape, bus windows fogged-over from all the human breathing,

lovers, masturbators, numb frostbit moon going black around the edges,

so many stops along the way, boarded-up gas stations and stores, caution

light swinging, butchered deer hanging head-down from maple branches,

crust of ice on blue snow radiant, some hollow-eyed chump embarking

from or disembarking into godforsaken loneliness which I had come

to love, not the lonely ones but loneliness itself, when I reached my stop

on Highway 2 outside Jack's, wild blueberry pie but closed, driver opened

the hatch and told me to crawl into the belly of the bus to retrieve my bag,

exhaust lit red when it pulled away, walked far that night, then through

hip-deep snow to the shack, no heat but wood, Faulkner and a feather bed.

I have slept in many places, for years on mattresses that entered

my life via nothing but luck, as a child on wet sheets, I could not

contain myself, as a teen on the bed where my father ate his last

pomegranate, among crickets and chicken bones in ditches, in the bare

grass on the lavish grounds of a crumbling castle, in a flapping German

circus tent, in a lean-to, my head on the belly of a sick calf, in a terrible

darkness where a shrew tried to stay afloat in a bucket of well water,

in a blue belfry, on a pink couch being eaten from the inside by field mice,

on bare floorboards by TV light with Mikel on Locust Place, on an amber

throne of cockroach casings, on a carpet of needles from a cemetery pine,

in a clubhouse circled by crabapple trees with high school boys who are

now members of a megachurch, in a hotel bathtub in St. Augustine after

a sip from the Fountain of Youth, cold on a cliff's edge, passed out cold

on train tracks, in a hospital bed holding my lamb like an army of lilacs.

My first night in New York, I was such a beautiful

dick, my soul circumcised, no shielding foreskin,

wearing some sort of leotard thing and gold fabric

safety pinned around my waist as a skirt, I'd pierced

one of my ears with a darning needle, ice cube

to numb it, to hurt: the only verb I knew, stabbed

through that ear hole a gold safety pin, the kind girls

back then wore on plaid skirts, and Kev that first night,

his robe an evil green, his unacceptable glamorous

nose, eyeholes as if precisely cut from his face

with a utility knife to exhibit the dangerous spectacle

at play inside his skull, Roland Barthes: "I cannot get over

having had this good fortune: to meet what matches my

desire," and, I would add, he who would slaughter me.

I'm watching *A Face in the Crowd* (1957), the scene

where Patricia Neal meets Lonesome Rhodes' first

wife played by Kay Medford, there's something about

the situation between the two women that feels so familiar

it rattles me, sitting here watching the scene, too, I've

done it before, done it a thousand times, Lee Remick

as the cheerleader wrapping her leg around Andy

Griffith's calf and Patricia Neal left in the lurch, her

deep-voiced drawl, I've been there, sat here, watched

that, felt this, like the first time I went to Little Szechuan

on Oliver St., the waiters washing the tables with hot

tea, whole fish in front of me, Kev plucking out the eye

with chopsticks and holding it toward me, my open

mouth in the mirrored walls a thousand times retold.

I can't rest, can't get no relief from fragments

of a life that come at me like pages in a flipbook,

like Hazel who walked by our house every day

in her black coat and veil and four-buckle Arctic

boots to head up Cemetery Lane to talk to her dead,

her parents, the fiancé who died in war, does she

matter, does the fact that I followed her and listened in

matter, or that a sonnet is one frame in a long strip

of celluloid most of which will end up on the cutting-

room floor back when there were cutting rooms as when

Kev who is long dead worked on *Radar Angel* editing

on the Steenbeck, I was OK-looking then, long hair dyed

blue, white dress, no idea who I was or what to be,

eating whipped cream in slow motion from a teaspoon.

I should have been in cinema. I should have been in paint

or founded a band. I am certain of nothing said the tattoo.

Where is home scratched the chickens. I should have met

the Stones when I had the chance. Should have let Keith

turn me inside out. So what if I ended up dead or crazy.

I am big but this feeling is bigger the silo whispered. I am

a movie screen drawled the pasture. I should have kept

the baby. So what poverty. I could have loved the little

fox-faced punk. I am buxom breathed the prairie. I should

have taken the radical path. I should have gone the cheerleader's

way. Should have married Chuck before he enlisted. What if

I'm a star said the lamb. A star said the ham. A star said

the duck. A star said the truck. A star said the star. Is this music

about sound and not notes. What if it broadcasts a shimmering.

Parties among strangers, punks, leather caps and straps, pressing

Quaaludes between my lips. What was pressed in I swallowed.

Is it hard for you to imagine me wearing gold lipstick? I did. Is it hard

for you to imagine me stupid? I was passed like bread among strangers.

For a couple of nights, I was the new thing. Then just a thing. Days I ran

a vintage clothing store, sat at a card table with a cigar box for a cash

drawer, the place too small for more than a couple of racks of old dresses

and tuxedos. Every day a screenwriter newly arrived from Poland sat

across from me, knee to knee, and read from his horrible screenplay.

He asked for critique, but when I gave it he derided me, once even spit

in my face. I quit the job to get away from him, or didn't quit, just didn't

show up one day. That's how things worked back then. I was valueless, no?

It seems strange now, when everyone is so intent on having value. I flitted

in my stolen vintage clothes, topless. I was that writer named anonymous.

There's something to be said for having one plate, one spoon,

a fork, a dull knife, living out of a red suitcase, eating when

hungry, grabbing shut-eye when tired, you're high-natured,

Joyce James said to me when I lived in NYC, we were in a cab

on our Friday lunch break going to a record store, decades later

I see I was not high-natured, only wanted love, though what that

means I don't know, something about mystery, standing humbly

at the gate of someone else's mystery and hoping for the sound,

at least now and then, of the hinges turning, mystery now,

mystery then, as when I went up to a guy at the record store

to ask him who did the song "Refugee" and he said, "Me,"

and I realized after I found the album and looked at the photo

on the cover I'd asked Tom Petty who did a Tom Petty tune

I'd heard on the radio when I was hungry and tired and alone.

Margaret Sanger did the first one, I was awake and felt terribly sorry

for myself, then when I didn't learn my lesson, for I was dumb and hazy

about how babies were made and, girl, I needed love, I set up the second one

with the breezy efficiency of Mr. Drysdale's secretary on *The Beverly Hillbillies*,

I'm going to do it right this time, I actually said that out loud, and borrowed

some dough so I could be knocked out cold and wouldn't have to feel anything,

the medical staff was young and encouraging with good teeth like members

of a college vocal jazz ensemble with an optimistic setlist, and they gave us

cookies when the anesthesia wore off, those crisp little butter cookies

with a hole in the middle, my eyes were like a cat's, they were actually as round

as dimes but I created the illusion of a cat with liquid eyeliner, I once stabbed

myself in the eye with the wand, what an awful mother I would have been, girl,

I was so loused up I didn't even grasp how lucky they were, those fairy-tale

urchins who could scrape themselves free of me and not end up in jail.

I saw Robert Creeley, I think it was on 8th St. near University Place. He wasn't wearing his glass eye. Did he even have a glass eye by then? If a person gives up on their glass eye, what do they do with it? Did he wrap it in a hankie and stick it in a drawer? Creeley didn't even waste his time on vowels. He spelled "said" this way: sd. I'd like to say we had a conversation, but we didn't. I had quite an interaction with Kenneth which involved him yanking out half my hair. My grandmother had a drawer for hankies. She rarely took the cloth ones from their narrow, smooth-sliding drawer. She loaned me one for my dad's funeral, just in case. My grandfather had a glass eye. He lost his real one as a boy, to a fishhook. Creeley lost his at age two in a freak accident "involving flying glass." Bart lost his eye to shrapnel at a construction site. He'd take out the glass one to entertain us kids. At three, I stepped barefoot on a rusty nail and said now I know how Jesus feels. A neighbor had a white bulldog, Rocko, with a missing eye. They make glass eyes for dogs but Rocko's people couldn't afford one. Rocko ambled around town like Creeley did that day in the Village with an empty socket.

The famous poets came for us they came on us or some of us

at least on some of us they did not come their poems were beautiful

or not but either way we learned to call them beautiful they came

like honeybees to hyacinths to some of us they came in some of us

the ones they called unreadable but fuckable or readable and fuckable

others were unfuckable the flip the fat the fierce the frayed the flawed

the frail the flunky the funny-looking radical unshaved the frumps

the flabs the poets came for us their genius sprayed on us they preyed

on us they said they'd pray for us like honeybees they dumped their load

of gold on us like god they shot their wad on us they called us sweeter

than their wives with softer skin they called their wives by telephone

their hands over our mouths to muffle us they shuffled us like decks

of playing cards and settled into hotel beds their socks and underwear

and undershirts cast upon the shore and then we'd stumble out the door.

Yes, I saw them all, saw them, met some, Richard Hell,

Lou Reed, Basquiat, Warhol, Burroughs, Kenneth Koch,

and it all left me feeling invisible or fucked, fucked

sideways, fucked by a john who stiffs you on your fee

and doesn't leave a tip, it wasn't impressive, it wasn't literary,

it wasn't titillating, I hope you are not titillated by it, their loathing

of women was indisputable, sometimes leaving genuine bruises,

more often just a sneer or no eye contact, the eyes wandering

off like dogs looking for something worth peeing on, or rarely

but potently and maybe worst of all something involving the word

beautiful, weaponizing the word beautiful, finally I took a turn

and made myself appalling, like drag queens and anorexics, I did

not want to be acceptable, I wanted to be alarming, hulk, colossus,

freak, maybe not a great life plan but a step in the right direction.

I can't say I loved punk when punk was contagious, CBGB nearly every night

at the behest of my boyfriend, Mudd Club, I lived within punk's borders,

there was no escape from its thesis, it manifested in style and music everything

that was unfolding in my daily life, chaos, rage, snot, vomit, junk, dissonance,

black eyes, noise unmediated by music, it was no more liberated than what

had come before and what had come before that, face it, jazz was the liberation,

the blues was liberation, the rest was the same old dangerous white boy song

and dance, unaware of its misogyny and convinced that its dangers were innovational

and had the power to uncap the revolution which, had it come, would have proven

to be a profound disappointment for they would have lost their supremacy, their

faux fiery crowns, even decades later when I had a chance to maybe hook up

with Jello after his monologue concert, I found myself unable to sit through

the oxygen-robbing eternity of his diatribe and left early, I heard he ended the night

eating pancakes just off I-94 at a Denny's on the east side of Kalamazoo.

Thirty-nine years ago is nothing, nothing. A three and a nine, nothing.

I had nothing left, a few clothes, some blousy trifles that mean nothing,

bangles left behind worth nothing, nowhere to live, sacking out trying

to sleep on my mother's couch, the touch of a bed too much, I had been

so hooked that nothing could hush my jones, Reagan elected, world

I thought I understood spun to nothing, Lennon blown to nothing,

not long before I'd bought a cherry popsicle right outside the Dakota,

lips cold and red, melted down to nothing, now every cell shivered

to return to 7th St., window looking out on gray nothing. It would be better,

I thought, if Kev had followed through and offed me like his hero William

Burroughs rather than this ostracism, though I was the one who left,

my mother had discharged her warhead, *if your father was alive*, against which

I was nothing, I knew nothing then of nothing, its shacks shawled

with moss, its bitter curatives and ancient hags redressing my narratives.

We all have our trauma nadir, the umbilicus from which

everything originates and is tied off and turns black

and the cord eventually falls away, to speak of it in mixed

company, well, it's just not done, to think of it alone,

in a one-room house with three of the four walls composed

of windows looking out onto bears, prehistory, don't think

of it alone, there is really no place for it, where do you

find an urn large enough to hold the ashes of a pod

of problematic blue whales, and even if you find that urn,

where is the mantel strong enough to display it, I do not

recommend home cremation, even of something as small

as a songbird, well, he burst into my bedroom, I was finally

asleep, I tried to kill myself, he said, and as I called for an

ambulance, he hacked away at his wrists with a pair of scissors.

I aborted two daughters, how do I know they were girls,

a mother knows, at least one daughter, maybe one

daughter and a son, will it hurt, I asked the pre-abortion

lady and she said, her eyes were so level, I haven't been

stupid enough to need to find out, cruel but she was right,

I was and am stupid, please no politics, I've never gotten

over it, no I don't regret it, two girls with a stupid penniless

mother and a drug-addict father, I don't think so, I shot

a rabbit once for food, I am not pristine, I am not good,

I am in no way Jesus, I am in no way even the bad Mary

let alone the good, though I have held my living son

in the pietà pose, I didn't know at the time I was doing it

but now that I look back, he'd overdosed and nearly died,

my heart, he said, his lips blue, don't worry, I've paid.

I fell on an incline, talus, tibia, fibula, calcaneal tendon mangled,

red circuits ruptured, body facing east toward a little town named

Climax and then New York where I once danced in a circle of girls

at Kev's sister's wedding, broom, shattered glass, Kev in his parents'

bathroom pilfering benzos from the medicine chest and now his

grave, lonely in sunlight in Sag Harbor, my leg twisted west toward

the lake, sunset, San Francisco where Mikel covered in KS lesions

with his last 50 bucks took me in a cab to see the Conservatory of Flowers,

actually only the zinnias, "just look," he said, a yellow that made my eyes

ache but nothing thus far compares to bone pain except childbirth,

put a bullet, I begged my ex-husband in the 48th hour of labor,

right here, pointing to my temple, leg inert in a black cast for months,

dead grandma's wheelchair, son by then a junkie, blank and mean,

I crawled to the cold road pleading for help, humbled yet, queen?

There is a force that breaks the body, inevitable,

the by-product is pain, unexceptional as a rain

gauge, which has become arcane, rhyme, likewise,

unless it's assonant or internal injury, gloom, joy,

which is also a dish soap, but not the one that rids

seabirds of oil from wrecked tankers, that's Dawn,

which should change its name to Dusk, irony being

the flip side of sentimentality here in the Iron Age,

ironing out the kinks in despair, turning it to hairdo

from hair, *to do*, vexing infinitive, much better to be

pain's host, body of Christ as opposed to the Holy

Ghost, when I have been suffering at times I could

step away from it by embracing it, a blues thing,

a John Donne thing, divest by wrestling, then sing.

It's that time of spring when the mulch ads come and so I remember cedar

mulch that smelled like a hope chest pine mulch dyed the color of hair dyed

bright red and the year my ex bought cocoa bean mulch and our lives smelled

like Hershey Pennsylvania I guess those are the things I didn't appreciate

enough I appreciated other things like when he remembered to pick up

the baby from day care but I digress I think there's still half a bag of mulch

in the garage which is damp since baby by then a teenager shot out the windows

and a squirrel with his BB gun and now that he's a man he still talks about hating

himself for the squirrel that was the year after his father left the same year I

think he was thirteen he spray-painted "Angelina Jolie" in purple on a big piece

of plywood and leaned it against the stone wall where as a toddler he'd stuck

the little glass animals that used to come in Red Rose tea boxes into gaps

between the stones but once his father was gone the mulch was gone

and then heroin and meth and crack and weeds and Angelina in the garden.

OD'd on his suboxone and not on purpose, opened in the kitchen dark a bottle

I thought was my own trifling med and took his drug instead, stop signs he called them,

helps you stop without insane withdrawal, but tells me now he just used it to deepen

his high, heighten his depths, he didn't care what he took or did or what combo

he imbibed, just ate up anything to make it better. Deader. I had no clue what I'd done

until later in bed my Self began to break into parts of equal measure like frames of film

unspliced and floating away from each other, alone, couldn't figure out how to use

the phone to call for help or to swallow my own spit, three days I sat up on the sofa

for fear of disremembering to breathe if I slept, him gone, out of his mind on dope

he tells me now, too hot for long sleeves and his arms covered in tracks so he

wouldn't come home for fear I'd see. On the third day, I returned to myself though

never all the way for I had glimpsed the oblivion he sought hourly for years, saw

I'd authored him in my bones, he was my allegory, analogy, corollary, mirror, I forged

his suffering, his nail, his needle, his thrill. Of course I swallowed the stupid pill.

Freelance artist. That's what you say when someone asks, "What do you do?" You've got to

back pocket. "What kind of art do you do?" Oh, this and that. Landscapes. Lots of landsc

disability—especially if they can't see anything wrong with you, no missing limb or visibl

want to work? Wouldn't you feel better if you did something with your life?" As if I woulc

doesn't want to be respectable. Leg blown off, yeah, that's pain. If your life is your pain, if

all the time, anxiety, dread, regret, guilt, there's no prescription for that. Not really. You ta

hope with each new prescription that doesn't fix a thing. You can get a wooden leg. They c

You can't cut out the part of yourself that doesn't work right. You can't get a wooden brair

in order to numb the pain. You do things that you wouldn't do under normal conditions.

but destroy you in the long run, like the reason you're on disability is made worse by being

that I'm suffering, but at the same time I want them to see me as a normal person. So whe

feel like this person recognizes that I'm something Other but still deserving of sympathy. I

called a human being. Sometimes I want to be looked at as a freak. I want people to stare

expect me to be normal. I can't live up to normal. Sometimes I embrace it. I embrace the t

I did, from my son's basement apartment, they'd come to feast off of what was left

was on the bottom floor, and no light, or very little light, there was a girlfriend,

y were into all things Russian, and the girlfriend didn't believe in housetraining dogs,

d out, took the few things of value and left behind a concrete floor full of dog shit,

had to cut me open, don't knock me out I yelled, after all this I want to be awake

lood, his hands looked too large for his body, and he spread them out, and his arms,

ke two bad teeth, and I didn't have to use my hands, the smoke from the crack draped

it was their house, half-smiling like I was selling Girl Scout cookies, but what the hell

tentionally made keen like a hawk's, I ordered them out, I threw their stuff in the yard, in

f summer, they rode away on bikes like children, like my sister and me when we

nees, riding our bikes through that water which must have been full of shit, my son,

e showed up at my house and put his hands on me, he didn't hurt me but it was

back legs and roared, I excommunicated him, hoisted him, my will by then was

for my touch is what I'm saying, don't ask me now to walk among the people.

I hoisted them, two drug dealers, I guess that's what they were, crackheads, I exiled them is what

of him, his entrails I guess, he'd moved into that apartment with such high hopes even though it

she moved in with her two dogs and then they picked up a stray pit bull they named Svetlana, th

like making them go outside in the yard was hurting their feelings or something, well she'd mov

and he, my son, I gave birth to him in 1985, it was a hard labor in a small-town hospital and they

when you lift out the kid, and I was, I was awake and they lifted him out, his skin painted with

well, all babies wail so he wailed, and I hoisted those two dealers, I excised them, I pulled them l

in their hair like cobwebs, I knocked on that black metal door, I knocked and they answered like

they were fucked up, they didn't know any better and with my voice alone, with my eyes that I i

the rain, dog shit was everywhere, like pine cones or apples in an abandoned orchard at the end c

were kids after a big storm and the drains were clogged on the streets so the water was up to our

he was nowhere to be found, I didn't see him until, what was it, later that night or the next day, l

moving in that direction, and something in me rose up, like a deer I once saw that stood up on it

like a jackhammer or a god, or one of those queens who wears a dress made of stone, so don't ask

have that ready to pull out of your

pes. If you tell the truth—I'm on

twitches or tics, you get, "Don't you

't want a job. As if any person

ou go through your days feeling fear

e the doctor's little pills. A bit less

n fasten you together with screws.

So you do stupid things to yourself

hings that make it better for a while

on disability. I want people to know

I go pick up a sandwich I want to

ot empathy, sympathy. Of being

me like that. So that they don't

le. Disability. That's what I am.

How do you stand being so virtuous? My only virtue is my lack

of virtue. My only fear my fear of a virtuous mob. Once my son sawed

through his wrists with a pair of scissors. Burst into my bedroom, I was

sleeping a rare sleep, dreaming a rare dream, and he cried that he had tried

to kill himself. Even as I called for help he sawed away. He was fucked up,

drunk, he knocked the phone out of my hand, maybe I slapped him,

he says I slapped him and I believe him. They sent him home after they

stitched up his wrists, wouldn't even keep him for a 24-hour hold. I made

threats, pulled rank. I'm a social worker, I yelled. Oh. Well then. Ha. He's still

got the scars. I saw them when we were playing Scattergories. For a while, I hid

everything sharp in the house. Even pencils and paring knives. But you can't

really live without sharp things. "If I want them I'll find them," he told me.

I use the scissors now to cut my bangs. One clean slice straight across my

forehead. Through virtue's flimsy yellow curtains there are many rooms.

Where is the drug to drug this feeling out of me, the drug

to drug away the fear of drugs and what they steal from me

or stole from me, sometimes love and then my sanity, the frozen

bowling ball that set up shop inside my gut and liked it there

and never went away, I never went away for fear of losing

what I left which was itself a kind of hell, the hell of being

terrified of swapping hell for hell, my son, fucked up, rolled

his car in dark Ohio, lay inside the ditch and listened to the crickets,

even grass, he said to me, he could hear it growing, and corn, all

of it just trying to get by, as close as he could come, he said, to God,

and I was such a fool, believing in fruition, stuck inside the fairy

tale of resurrection, even stars, he said, are trying to get by and then

he used for ten more years and bankruptcy and where's the melody

to remedy the melody, the remedy to remedy the remedy?

Then, I account it high time to get to sea as soon as I can, he says,

quoting *Moby-Dick*. I'm tired of a sedentary life, he tells me. I'm ready

to knock people's hats off in the street, again paraphrasing Melville.

The sea is a place to go when your mind wanders so much that you'd

like a place to be able to look around and think or say, I can't wander

anymore. What is a dog, he says, if not the whole sea? One dog is a giant

in comparison with the lot of seas. Why don't you get a dog, I ask. I'm not

the caliber of person who has the capacity to take care of a dog, he tells me,

and there's no arguing it. I miss shooting dope so much, he says. I'd never

do it again because my heart would give out but I miss it. I'd never do it.

I want to live. I like it here. I like living here with what I have. This apartment.

The lake. The relative solitude. The cold when it gets here. The sounds

of the ships. That is a very short list, I realize, he says. I must go to sea,

he says. But I've been to sea (a very little). And I still feel no contentment.

Which, he asks me, is your favorite story of Jesus, and I tell him walking on water,

what is yours, and he tells me when Jesus fucks up the temple, it's cool, he says,

when Jesus flips, or maybe when Jesus says on the cross he thirsts but rejects the bad

vinegar, what about the Garden of Gethsemane, I ask him and he says, I just feel angry

about the Garden, he told them what to do, he goes a stone's throw away to pray

and repeatedly says some of the most beautiful things, and they still mess up, if Jesus

tells me to chill but stay awake I'm gonna chill and stay awake, I mean find the middle

ground, he tells them to chill out, don't flip, don't fall asleep, but then he comes back

after he's been praying to his Father and they are asleep, Jesus told them to stay awake

with him but rest, if Jesus told me to rest I would rest so well, I mean I'm goddamned

tired, but I wouldn't fall asleep on him, FYI, he says, he told them to stay awake

with him, stay with the goddamned Lord, and he repeatedly prays beautiful words,

he sweats blood, his face in the dirt, and twice they fell asleep on him like a trio of drunks,

which makes one wonder about the Lord's judgment in choosing his goddamned friends.

She's a big James Stewart fan, he says, but she hates my

impression of him. Hates my Clinton impression, Bill

not Hillary, hates my Obama impression, doesn't know

who Rodney Dangerfield is but still hates it, hates my Kurt

Russell in *The Thing*, hates when I do Jack Nicholson talking

about how great his hot tub is, hates my Al Pacino the most,

she just gets mad, he says, and I tell him, don't do impressions

then, it's probably not worth pissing her off, the only one

she likes, he says, is my Don Corleone, she likes how I add in

things about him wanting food, chips, dip, pizza rolls, sloppy

joes, just Don Corleone demanding junk food, that's the whole

impression, basically just a real-life late-stage Marlon Brando,

I came up with a Dennis Hopper but haven't performed

that one for her yet, that one, he says, is almost too easy.

Why would God be so mean, he asks, expecting no answer. Who is this person who

wrote the Old Testament? Must have been a testy individual. Always smiting this

and that. I don't know why but I think of Jesus as the guy in the paintings, the classic,

he says. Long blond hair, piercing blue eyes, little goatee. I know that isn't factual

but I can't get over the paintings. Sounds like an alien, I say. That's what he was

in many ways, he says. He just floated on up to the sky after revisiting his disciples

and whatnot. I wonder if Jesus wants souls like the devil does. You know, are they

engaged in a competition. I wonder if the Lord forgives people who are mean

to their mother, he says. Because I've been mean. Was also wondering if when Jesus

was asking if the cup could be passed if he already knew the answer. What is the best

song with Jesus in the lyrics, he asks. I like when Nirvana did "Jesus Doesn't Want Me

for a Sunbeam," he says. Well, either way, I always think Jesus will shore it all up, he says.

What are you reading these days, I ask, trying to change the subject. I read the Bible

a lot, he says. I like John. You can tell he's making it all up but the writing's good.

Then when I grew up I became one of those, what's one of those, I ask, one of those men who rides women around on their shoulders at parties, at beaches, I did a lot of dumb stuff with women, you learn to carry them around, feed them like a child, to earn them, to be reputable, a reputable man, I used to be such a player, he says, in the game, horrible, but all in all it was better than these last 12 years or however long it's been, now I just listen to country western music, "well I've been kicked by the wind, robbed by the sleet / had my head stoved in, but I'm still on my feet / and I'm still willin'," that's Lowell George, Little Feat, listen to it, he says, listen, it's enough, he says, but it doesn't feel like it, what do you mean, I ask, I'll write a country western song about it, he says, used to carry girls around on my back / now I sleep alone when I hit the sack / I been so poor and been outside / my woman left me and I can't even cry / I eat cracker sandwiches and wish I could die / I get in my pickup each day / doing work for almost no pay / sometimes I think I belong in a ditch / but I'll take another bite of this cracker sandwich, you don't want to die, I say, it is a song, he says, a song, not me, do I have a truck and a job, am I a grown man known to eat cracker sandwiches?

What do you think Elvis's best song was, he asks, for me, he says, it's that "Hunk of Burning Love" song, you can tell he's sad, he says, but he's really going for it, I hate that song, I say, I find it embarrassing, I prefer the earlier stuff, "Heartbreak Hotel," "Jailhouse Rock," those, so you're basically saying I'm stupid, he says, no, I say, I'm saying I like those two and don't like "Burning Love," you asked for my opinion, "Blue Moon" is better than those two, he says, and "Lawdy Miss Clawdy" from the comeback concert is better than "Blue Moon," and Elvis has some great Jesus songs, his Jesus songs are so flabby, I say, his Jesus songs are so purple, wack, he says, on the subject of Elvis you're wack, how about "Where Could I Go but to the Lord," have you listened to "Where Could I Go but to the Lord" lately, no, I say, I'm no aficionado, I am not an aficionado like you are on this subject and I never said I was, well, he says, I just cling to his later songs, why do you cling, I ask, I'm saying if you would just consider his situation and so on, he says, maybe you'd come to like "Burning Love," maybe you'd feel differently about "Burning Love."

On what day do you think Jesus was actually born, he asks,

and do you think Billy Idol is talented but dumb or smart

but talentless, I love the cold, he says, I love it to be as cold

as it can possibly be, I want snow as high as the rooftops,

which is why he swears he'll never come home from the north,

never back over the bridge, not for holidays like the false birthday

of the so-called Lord, throw out my stuff, all of it, he says, so

cold I can spit and it freezes, makes a *chhh* sound like Billy Idol

pronounces *s* when he's really rocking, did you see him live, he

asks, did you see the Clash, yes to the Clash, no to Billy, I spat

and it froze in November, he says, rare these days, never home, not

for funerals or to sleep in his old room where I used to find empty

quarts of vodka, needles, pipes, but he's clean now, clean, gorgeous

word like snow, like cold, if I were Jesus, he says, I'd make it colder.

Maybe we wander the soundless antechambers, halls
and gateways, rustling scapular and underskirt, slight
swinging of the cross on its cord makes a sound
like a bottle fly. Angular shadows, stories-tall, color
of Mourvèdre grapes, purple-black with a yeasty haze.
Maybe—can it be? Death is a nunnery? Six lines and sick
already of this allegory. Looking for a nonfussy definition
of the Sublime. Something I can really sink my teeth into
like the tough meat of an animal, the last of its kind. Or
spinning the wool of a black sheep, all the while telling
myself the story of myself. Nurse says the membrane
between life and death will thin like the effacement
of the cervix. I remember begging to die when I gave
birth and begging to be born when I was dying.

I've lived with death from the beginning, at the edge

of its villages. I sang it little songs, pried open its mildewed

pods until the seed fluff detonated in my face like, well you

know what it's like when seeds detonate in your face. I lived

so close to death I got inured to it all, like being so comfortable

living in the underground house we didn't notice the dirt walls

crawling with colonies of ants feeding their winged queens, or how

we got so used to living next to the train tracks that the screaming

whistle didn't wake us. I've known the echoes of death's amphibians

and the poems of its fine gentlemen with their monocles and top hats,

cravats and curls, their adverbs. I hate adverbs. I died but how

did I die? Swimmingly! Prettily! Open-throated Italian shirts,

white as eyeballs rolled back, cuff links and first-rate booze,

the green kind, green as heat lightning, as magic shoes.

I fell in love with death, he isn't mean, his kisses wet and sweet.

Broken pocket watch, strange chain, like an extra in a Western

who appears at the edge of the screen perched atop a lame horse.

Thinness at the hips, the incubator of his breath. Mother tongue

in his mouth. Kinky, but in the most earnest, heartfelt way: he

sucked my fingers while I read him *Peter Pan*, itself a children's book

about dead children. His only perversion is innocence, doesn't try

to ruin Christmas but ruins it anyway, young uncle in the disturbing

T-shirt who just can't get into the spirit of the holiday. *Try*, some

female relative whispers in his ear through her lipstick, just try.

He wipes away her kisses, disingenuousness not in his repertoire.

Can't fake it. If his eyes are hollow it's because he's feeling hollow.

If he's in the mood he calls me at twilight from some meadow,

describes how the sun digs its own grave, the copper afterglow.

I could do the love but I couldn't do the pyre, and here we go again, we'll slip

the hankie from the drawer and the macaroni salad from its hiding place and the pine

box or cherrywood or poplar with copper handles with or without grave liners

or the fire and the cardboard receptacle or handmade urn and the whoosh

of ashes into creek or estuary or off a ship or out of a plane and the blowback

and the minister with his trumpet or some screaming evangelical or gloomy rabbi

or agnostic eulogist, some meaning-maker with his Yeats or Keats or e. e. cummings,

all weird and no caps, at my father's I was small and sat on the floor of the hearse,

people said don't be sad, there was macaroni afterward, I liked macaroni, I got into

my grandma's medicine cabinet and squished some dark green toothpaste into the sink

and painted my fingernails red but no matter, I wore pink knee socks but never mind,

and now this, and one of us is going to have to listen to that banjo tune "Hand in Hand"

played by Tony Ellis on a rotten portable CD player at some chapel or graveside or crematory,

Tony Ellis while the body burns, how does that grab you, and now we're stuck with it.

I've encountered the exoskeleton of a book I wrote or poem

or word I passionately laid upon the page, the passion's gone,

the word looms, ambered, hunched, uncanny, dead-eyed, gold

light shines through it like a lithophane, I have wanted to dig up

the dead to see what's left, would almost rather meet the shell

than the soul, break the frozen ground, burial vault, box they house

them in which could be reduced to bronze handles, hinges, and screws,

the body just an armful of kindling or handful of blue fibers from

the designated suit, the list of pall bearers still in a drawer somewhere

and the alternates in case someone couldn't stomach bearing the corpse

from hearse to church and back to hearse and then to graveside, the story

played out in rectangular units like plant cells or jail cells of a career

criminal or Stations of the Cross or that multihued Jell-O concoction

called funeral salad or uniform rooms in a Bauhaus dollhouse.

All lives have their tropes over which we have minimal control. Maybe beauty

is your trope. That's a good one. Or maybe you're the ugly one. Not fun.

You feel the eyes and learn to live with them. Or you're the princess rankled

by the pea. Or the pea smothered under 10,000 mattresses and the princess

on top like a heavy cherry. Who am I to judge the framing of a life? What if birds

are it? All your birthday gifts bird-related. A special thing for red-haired ones

that peck ants out of dead trunks. Or earning abs and biceps, controlling

your relentless hungers, a closet full of tiny sleeveless dresses in all the pastel

shades of after-dinner mints. Maybe you're marked as maudlin, or the one

who marks others as maudlin with a big fat pen. Or a couple hundred years ago

your people were owned. Or your people owned people. Your people were burned.

Or your people lit the match. The evils wriggle through the generations

like corpse worms. My great-great-grandfather beat to death a plow horse

in a field of grain. No wonder everything since has reeked of peasantry and pain.

In the dream, my mother called my name from the lower levels, I called her

name from the uppermost level, not Mother, but the name she was stuck

with when she was born, she never liked it, nor her hair, called it bushy

but didn't really care, I take some comfort in her knowing I was there, the crowd

kept her from the climb, it wasn't in her nature to rise, slept on sugar sacks

in the cellar when she was a kid, from my vantage point I could see the whole

sky, the totality, horizon's circumference, funnel clouds of every ilk snaking

in our direction, when she was five she lied to the barber, said he was to cut

off her hair as short as a boy's, after the tornadoes hit I ran through the wreckage

to find her, the peasants on the lower levels had drowned, I called her name

again, loud, an old woman sat on a folding chair, humped like a witch, in charge

of the dead, my mother, my mother, the old woman pointed to a body in a line

of wet bodies on the floor, I screamed the scream of giving birth: she was what

I had, or all I had, or all I had *left*, it is hard to remember dialogue in dreams.

I dreamed of it again, my dad's body lost to us again but finally

found again, we set him in Dickinson's coffin, wooden, painted

white, where had his body been all these years, things felt strange,

I could see the stitches holding my dad's eyelids shut, but lo

and behold his eyelashes, so long they tangled now and then, were

still intact, and at his throat, like Emily's, a nosegay of violets,

a pink cypripedium, and two heliotropes in his hands, I loved

his hands, they were not large hands, they cut and sanded wood,

they had a fineness, a delicacy, it was said after Emily's little nephew

died she became delicate, would not even let the doctor feel her

pulse, just walked past the door so he could diagnose her via

a glance, my mother and sister added bluebells to his coffin

but they called them sweet peas, I don't know why, I don't

know why I miss Emily so, and him, why die, why dream?

I dreamed I had to find my way from the city where I live now

to the place I call my hometown, I had to ride a bike and night

was falling and to make things worse there had been flooding,

there was a flood, why in dreams do streams escape their borders,

why must I backtrack to keep myself from drowning, the alternate path

was dark and then I had to pee, squat on the side of the road among

the cattails and puzzlegrass, and lost my pants in the process, lost them

in the dark, there'd been a flood, I was wandering without pants between

the land of my earliest days and what I now call home, then came a man

in a truck, just my luck a man with a truck, a knife, and a dream, it was

a knife that could cut an ear of corn from its stalk, many ears from many

stalks, he saw that the road was dark, he saw the shadows of stalks

in the moonlight, and then he robbed me of my dream, it became his dream,

and like Lorca in "Rider's Song" I never made it back to the motherland.

Goldenrod, I could say, you know, everybody wants something

from me, but, well, everybody wants something and nobody wants

nothing from me, goldenrod, towhead, beast. Goldenrod, you pack

the meadows like gold-plated sardines. I have heart palpitations

but all forms of relief end with a kickback, like my aunt with the black

eye who lied she was kicked by a horse. Free goldfinch comes to feast

on thistles in May and perches and weaves and sings of its political

exhaustion. Pisses me off, bird, to find out the devil from Sunday school

is real. I didn't even have my own Sunday school. Trespassed and thieved

art supplies and gibberish. Had I only tied the play apron around my waist

and faced the windy sun and watched your gold hermaphroditic wands sway.

Dumbbell that I was I sought a product called God though the whole village

was opulent with gilded heathens. Goldenrod, is your dying hard? I know,

I know dying's hard. Are you reaching toward, you know, or just reaching?

How will I leave this life, like I left my job, drifting off without

comment, like mother took off to get schooled, shut the door

hard on my crying, she had books to read, or father in an ambulance,

rotating light swept red over oak trees, then the hospital bed,

hallucinating warship and sea, or the way my ex left us, dragging

his clothes in a garbage bag through snow like fresh kill, or like I left

Kev, I had twenty minutes before he'd get home to try to change my mind

or kill me, out the red door with my dad's briefcase full of all my poems

and the typewriter and seal-skin coat, and then the airplane home,

so freaked by the years with him in New York I broke when I stirred

up a grouse in the woods, will I leave like a grouse leaves, drumming

the air with its wings, or like Freddie left the stage when Queen played

Live Aid, glossed like a racehorse, top of his game, or like I leave parties,

no valedictions, out the door like smoke from extinguished candelabras.

I dreamed a color, no plot, a color, strange, there once

were shoes called oxblood, the color was akin to oxblood

baby shoes, but not that exactly, nor calves' liver, though

closer to liver than heart, nor that girl with oxblood hair,

nor mahogany, fuck mahogany, I fell once, walking on the rocks

along a jade lake, the cut was small but deep and mean, my

blood, magenta edged in something the color of antifreeze,

an unthinkable yellow-green, bioluminescent though not like

a glowworm, fuck glowworms, they lean toward the false indigo

of cheap illuminated wristwatches, maybe a certain bunch

of gladiolas delivered to my studio apartment by Mikel, who opened

my honey jar and licked all the way around its mouth, fuck that, it

incensed me, the color some combination of glads, honey, tongue,

rage, and Mikel, dead so long, the Kaposi's lesion on his thumb.

He called from San Francisco, I was nursing the baby, he said I have

a lesion on my calf, it looks like a cigarette burn, this was early in the plague,

no cocktail, my basement apartment beset with wasps, the nest located

in the bathroom fan, then biting red ants, basement no place for a baby,

looking back that part was small potatoes, I was nursing again when

the *Challenger* blew up, they say the astronauts were alive until the cabin hit

the water, eyes open all the way down, you'd think my milk would have been

copious but it was not and yet I am an animal, from there it was neuropathy

in his feet, he hobbled, who'd once won the town tennis tournament, three

figures wearing black showed up at the end of his bed, and he went blind,

thought the answer was dime-store reading glasses, his mind, gone, then his

body filled with ocean water though he was from a freshwater place, river,

stream, mucky inland lake, newts in the window wells, his parents were poor

but had scored a secondhand aboveground pool there behind the fruit stand.

I want to zero in on what he looked like, for posterity if nothing else, there was more

than a little bit of Nicholson in *Chinatown*, the hairline but not the toughness, not the hetero

gaze through half-closed eyes or the nasty gash on the nose that Nicholson wore through

most of the movie, though toward the end Mikel did have lesions on his nose and ear and neck

and temple, definitely some Neil Young, the mouth, the lowering of the chin and looking out

from behind the hair that fell over his eyes when he was very young, getting called a faggot

by the football boys, art class, we drew together, what I took for romantic interest was interest,

actual interest, and later when he was full-on dying he made complicated arrangements for me

to inherit his car to replace the piece of shit Oldsmobile I was driving, in the end his friend sold

his car in San Francisco and sent me a check to put toward a used Chevy Nova, maroon, scarred

but it ran OK, now and then he'd say, "I'm Suck Owens and these here boys are my Fuckaroos"

and sing "I've Got a Tiger by the Tail," but more often in his upstairs room on Locust Court he'd

play the piece of shit guitar, always such a light touch, sing "helpless, helpless, helpless, helpless,"

that song, mattress on the floor, I didn't mind, alarm clock on the windowsill, the windup kind.

He said it bummed him out his dick didn't work anymore.

But it was never about dick for us. Was it. Though for a while

it was all about dick for him. San Francisco dick. Far, far away

from his brutal fireman father. And me. He could finally do what

he wanted with his dick and other people's dicks. And dress as *I*

Love Lucy. And write a serial featuring Dyke Van Dick. And refer

to himself when not wearing dress and wig as an existential cowboy.

"The charismatic impresario of all we did," Alan said of him. But that

wasn't how it was for us. We did not waste our charisma on each other.

Did not dress for each other. Or did I dress for him a little bit. Did

I perform for him. I knew no other way. The last time I saw him.

Before he lost his mind and filled with ocean. Died. He said, "Di

your body changed." I'd just given birth to a ten pound baby. Jesus

Christ. What do you want from me. What did you ever want from me.

I saw a little movie of a person stroking a small bird with two Q-tips, one held between the forefinger and thumb of each hand. It tipped back its head to receive the minor tenderness, which to the bird must have felt like being touched by a god. For a moment I knew what it would be to feel at the mercy of love, small-scale, the kind shown but not spoken of. I was afraid to touch you. I was afraid of the lesions you'd described to me over the phone, their locations and the measurement, in centimeters, of each. Jesus-marks, you called them. All so I would be prepared and unafraid or less afraid but still I was afraid of dying like you were dying. When I first arrived I looked so long into your eyes you shivered and ordered me to look away. You were imperious in your dying yet courtly about my fear, you understood, as if I were a child afraid of lightning storms, which I am, having at age ten been struck. Out of the blue you said that once you were dead I'd never be able to listen to *Blue* again, Joni Mitchell's *Blue*, not just the song but the whole album. It was a minor curse you lay across my shoulders like a fur dyed blue, and so I listen now in defiance of you. In the listening the pronoun shifts. We are listening. There is no death.

Things feel partial. My love for things is partial. Mikel on his last legs, covered

in KS lesions demanded that I see the beauty of a mass of chrysanthemums. Look,

he demanded. I lied that I could see the beauty there but all I saw was a smear

of yellow flowers. I wanted to leave that place. I wanted to leave him to die

without me. And soon that's what I did. Even the molecule I allowed myself to feel

of our last goodbye made me scream. What would have happened if I'd opened

my heart all the way as I was told to do if I wanted Jesus to live inside one of its

dank chambers? Whitman told me to "Unscrew the locks from the doors! Unscrew

the doors themselves from their jambs!" Let love come streaming in like when

the St. Joe flooded Save A Lot and drove it out of business. The only store in town.

Don't put my ashes in the river, Mikel said. Put them in a tributary. I did. I put them

in a tributary without touching them. Now I want to chalk my fingerprints with them

but it's too late. I want to hold them like he held me and touched my upper lip and called it

Cupid's cusp, a phrase that made me wince. I felt love all the way then, and never since.

Death does not exist in poetry. A line may fade into the silence past its breaking

but that is not death. No choking sounds in poems, no smell of blood. I can describe

the sounds, the smells, but description is, in fact, a hiding place. There is no nobility

in description. Is there nobility in poems? Let's hope not. Nobility is another place

to hide. "Through all these myriad felt and mostly scorned and disreputable realities,"

Alan wrote in a poem. I hope it is OK that I have quoted you, Alan. It is a poem

about love's nuance but Alan would agree there is no love in poems. There is no love

in a mushroom, in a handmade wedding dress. No death in a funeral hankie

embroidered with the words "Try not to use it." I looked at a worm and I thought

it was an angel. I looked at an angel and thought it was a storm. What is wrong

with the mind is what is wrong with the poem. It is difficult to get the news-

boy to be a newsboy. He keeps turning into a girl carrying a fish in a cloth delivery

bag to her grandmother who is really a wolf dressed as a grandmother singing a line

from *Ulysses*: "So stood they there both awhile in wanhope, sorrowing one with other."

I was tethered to this Earth by just a few simple objects,

a tattered copy of *Dubliners*, especially the story where

the boy observes the dead body of the former priest, "his

face was very truculent, grey and massive, with black

cavernous nostrils and circled by a scanty white fur," a horse,

a memory of a horse, not even a ring, not even a house key,

and then the book was lost, stolen in an airport, I'd been

only halfway through the story "A Little Cloud," I recall

the last sentence I read: "Ignatius Gallaher took out a large

gold watch and looked at it," a good sentence, strong,

without which I was lost, effervesced, sky above me tarred

with a wide, clumsy brush, below thunderheads, saddlebags

of rain sliced by tridents of lightning, the book had been

saddle-colored, or the color of the animal beneath the saddle.

Abrupt lines on the nature of beauty: I've examined death

masks, most but Tesla's look the same, oh poor Lincoln

is Lincolnish, Franklin, doughy, Keats, who'd wake up

sobbing that he was still alive to agonize, beautiful, meaning

what, tender planes of his face, eyelashes, the narrative

of his suffering up against the imperturbability of the plaster

as if napping under a willow and a temperate breeze,

Fanny Brawne on his mind, of whom he wrote: "—her Arms

are good, her hands bad-ish," or is he beautiful because his

poems are beautiful and what is a beautiful poem, or his

face is serene unlike the old man whose mask captures

the vile contortions of the last gasp, I'd like to educate

myself about the beauty of *that*, Keats writes "Beauty

is truth," so in what dark closet hides Fanny's last face?

Literature is dangerous business, the entrapment of form in poetry, plot

in fiction, can be claustrophobic to a person like me, and no trellised exit gate,

one can find themselves not just lost but impaled on the tangible details

of someone else's world—blue paint drying on the pickets, meaty smell of hot

shrubbery—mere facsimiles, but also by the feelings of the characters, stratified,

as if by some eons-spanning organic process, grief, desperation, self-deception,

scattered sparingly with some gorgeous momentary wish fulfillment, two

characters, one secretive and impacted, one spontaneous, who meet at night

on a serpentine bridge, wordless brushing of fingertips over wrist, lips over jaw,

then part, headed for university or war, or their romance blossoms for a time

but goes flat, wrecked by capitalism, sex roles, time, you see, for weeks on end

I'm stuck in this prison made of paper and ink, this grinding ménage à trois,

unable to eat or drink, rereading those few sentences written by someone

wracked with syphilis that emit the pepper-scented musk of white Hesperis.

I wanted to be the boy in the book, the beautiful narrow fellow who stumbles

upon desire like a pebble along the footpath, I want to be that boy, nothing

extra on him, nothing built for nursing or bleeding or bearing someone like him

into the world, to see someone and want them and suffer over it, elegantly,

the beautiful suffering that desire offers up to us, that wanting is not having,

that having is not having always, that we can enter a body through its many

mouths but we cannot stay, there is no staying, to be a woman and to desire

with elegance has been for me impossible, to be a girl stumbling upon desire

like a rock along the footpath meant falling clumsily and breaking like a mirror,

to be a man, I think to be a man is its own sinkhole, I would be a boy, this boy,

a literary boy made of literature not flesh, this heroic fool impaled on desire

cleanly as on a pearl-handled knife, illicit desire, all desire should be illicit, its

fulfillment transpiring in wet, blue-shadowed places where a life like a shirt comes

undone, for me, it's too late to be this boy lusting for the man he will become.

My literary tastes of late are manic, Hopkins, the complete Grimm's, just now "The Shoes

That Were Danced to Pieces," Chekhov's notebooks, and on TV a Hitchcock episode about

a murderous ventriloquist and Riabouchinska, the dummy he loves, a woman puppet

who wears a crown, I move from novel to story to Chekhov's precious but banal ramblings,

"the wife of the engineer Gliebov, who has been killed hunting, was there. She sang a great

deal," to a current novel, this one I read on a small apparatus with a screen on which one

turns virtual pages, and is most directly about doomed love, that's the through line of all

my selections, and then my sonnet begins to speak back to me, it is my lone companion, my

absinthe drinker, my crowned confidante, why, it asks, do you leap madly from text to text,

and I tell my sonnet of leaping from my own bed to my sister's when the doctor made a house

call to inject me with a vaccine, bed to bed to escape his serum, "Do you want typhoid fever?"

he shouted, but I leaped, imagining myself royalty who fled the king through a passageway

under my bed where my prince waited in a boat to carry me to the ball where I would dance

holes in my shoes and sing a great deal, then die of typhoid fever, like Gerard Hopkins.

Chekhov sits waiting for me at the kitchen table, tea growing cold,

although I promised myself, I can't lift the heavy orange book, maybe

because Richard selected the stories for this edition and I met him

once, his suitcase packed with military precision, and I made a kind

of fool of myself, darting off to retrieve his forgotten hotel key

like I was his amanuensis, or because my son loves Chekhov and now

lives far north, says he will never return, to throw out everything

but the wooden camera he built, installing the glass lens nearly killed him,

or that Carver story "Errand" about Chekhov's last days, "She stayed

with Chekhov until daybreak, when thrushes began to call from the garden

below," there are times one needs to read nothing at all, stare at birds,

play solitaire, but then I discover a dead one, a bird, which must be tended to,

buried, my neighbor finds its black leg and foot detached from the body,

throws it in the hole along with a handful of stiff blue feathers.

Either all of this is an apparition or I am, and where the apparition

began I don't rightly know, maybe I'm still coupled, maybe I have

a towhead in tow, my singularity in every circumstance a mirage,

reading *Dubliners* at Orlando's eating a taco while the whole

world sips its margaritas in tandem, watching a meteor shower

from a blue picnic table in the dark near a tributary of the Rio

Grande, wild dogs rambling through the pueblo beneath the Blood

of Christ mountains where I will never belong nor should I,

and magpies with the indigo feathers down their backs

who can recognize their own faces in looking glasses, or Intro

to Buddhism, peyote-tripping through class, the prof spinning

a prayer wheel like a party favor, maybe all the way back to being

trapped with my dad in a House of Mirrors, reaching for a father

and banging into glass, self, self, impairment, hallucination.

Mountains black today, hiding when the wind cooperates behind Whitman

beards, legless homeless talking to themselves on red dirt corners, laughing

at the nothing there is to laugh at, holding up blank cardboard signs,

the want so great they can't put words to it, and I belong nowhere, have

never belonged anywhere, not where I was raised, not where I was not raised,

not in any classroom or strip motel or restaurant of any false or real ethnicity,

not chic, not invisible, not urban but no farm where my apron can flap

in the wind, not in any workplace, my God, workplaces, I know this

is the wail of a teenager and yet I'm not really wailing, am I, am I wailing,

I'm saying this body has never been a home, my shack a shackle, dog

is a good boy but he bites, poems are someone else's clothes I slipped

into so I could skip town, even the hospital where I was born was borrowed

from the Catholics, nuns thought I was odd and tried to foist me off

on the Buddhists but they reached through the fog and handed me back.

For twenty-six days I lived in an apartment with a dishwasher,

and I'll tell you, it changed me, it changed my hands not to have

them daily in hot, soapy water, and the change wormed its way

up my arms all the way to my brain, so that I became incredulous

at the notion of ever having worked through a sink full of dishes,

I was also in a strange time zone, and at a high elevation, so that

in bed, flat on my back, I felt short of breath like an invalid, I was

like Keats, and cried a little upon waking as he did, opening

his eyes once again to dying, and people in the town treated me

with an unaccustomed degree of respect, when they shook

my hand I could tell they were thinking that it was soft,

and it was soft, so was my other hand, the softness snaked

everywhere, into all the corners of my life and my whole interior,

I had no origin story, no soul, I was, practically speaking, an appliance.

When I am away I miss my ravaged hovel and its birds

pecking at the house like a boy in speckled trousers

nibbling on the witch's sugared windowpanes I miss the sky

dustrag at dawn menstrual rag at sundown and my mother

who takes a lawn chair to the cemetery so she can rest

from tending graves and watches a field mouse poke up

from a hole next to my father's grave and a snake unwind

itself from her parents' shared stone and a flock of wild

turkeys humped beneath their shawls of feathers squandering

their lives beneath the trees and notices a trampled path

from the woods to meadow where the deer run

and single-file cross over our future graves she bought

the plots cheap one year and an urn for her own ashes

from the mortician who has loved her for years from afar.

It's a real Garden of Eden story, the mother of the little

compound, founder, embracer, died of cancer, then some

goof from Arkansas moved in thinking he could plant corn

after they told him you can't plant corn in the mountains,

there will be a freeze on one end or the other, planted corn,

it froze, and now he's out there most nights burning husks

for God knows what purpose, and he's got keep-out signs

all over the range so Shawn can't walk his dogs out there

and the half-coyote Rico sits smack in front of Shawn and stares

into his eyes like hypnotism, but you know how coyotes are,

that high laugh-cry that throws salt into your wound at the time

of night you're already bedded down in your loneliness,

and Arkansas out there setting fires and the dry trees rattling

their leaves like some golden currency no one uses anymore.

And then landscape was all there was. Curves of rock blocking

the sky like drive-in movie screens showing repeatedly films about

ribbons. Breast-shaped blood-colored towers. Beautiful, my mind

called it. I languaged it so I wouldn't have to hear the wind. Two

weeks in a hotel off the interstate. So lonely I started getting mawkish

about other people's fingerprints on the headboard, hawkish about

hawks. Do hawks eat roadkill? What eats hawks? I turned encyclopedia

into a verb. Ate every meal at Dick's. Who's Dick, I asked the waitress.

Nobody remembers the original Dick. They'd been looking to hire

a Dick but so far no applicants. I need my loneliness, I was quoted

as saying. Someone writing the narrative called me a ribbon-snipper.

I don't have a zip code, a house, a dog, mailman, milkman, president,

dad. It's a classic Western tableau: man wearing a hat under a derelict

sky. Not a cloud in the. In this case, a bitch wearing a fedora.

The emergent self is not a self that loves. Love

unlasting. Love, unlasting as a sentence. One feels

love's depths, and yet its depths are shallow. Something

beneath the shallows, and something beneath that.

Darkness guarded by air-raid curtains. Not ennui.

Don't pin that on my lapel. Sublimity. Basement

of an infinite underworld museum where, in secret,

death and the sublime bash against each other as clouds

bash during storms, or theories bash in rooms full

of theoreticians. Love, having felt it, one wonders how

it can be a rather small thing, yet if it were in the sky,

it would be the wing of some dumb flying machine

blushed for a moment like a tangerine but remember

the sky's largesse and emptiness, and larger still, the self.

Takes time to get to minimalism, years lived through, eau de

suffering, yes, I'm in that camp, as Orr writes, we move from

choked silence to blurted speech to diary with its useless key

to story to poetry, the most shaped, therefore most distant from

the original crime, even pleasure can be a crime, especially

once it's lost, and happiness, the word an assault on the tongue,

why, the patient asks the doctor, does everything taste bitter

as the stems of dandelions, even the tongue tasting itself tastes

bitter. When I was a child, one night, all I could smell was blood,

I told no one, it went on like that for months until a torrential rain

laundered the air, Con at 88, his lungs full of cancer, mind hijacked

by dementia, can't remember his own poems nor holding a pen,

though he accepts my reading them to him, that's a good one, he

says, coughs, an urn-shaped moment, thus radiant, therefore true.

All things now remind me of what love used to be. Swollen cattails in lonely

places. Gluey conditioner in my hair. Firm books. Their variegated spines.

Swirl of words like a stirred cocktail, whirled umbilicus, pulsing asterisk.

The past is this: to have been young and desirous and to be those things

no more. In the future the cattails will explode without me. I pray they will

not go unseen. Who will ride the cemetery horses? Incorrigible blond forelocks

blowing in their eyes. Back when I walked through cemeteries commenting

on the strange names. The present tense: to take a loveless path is to court

a purple-blue emptiness, like a disco or a grotto. Or the cave where dead bodies

are stored in the winter, when a shovel can't break through frozen ground.

I have seen such spaces. I have been alone in them. Sound of water lapping.

Animals calling to each other. Echo of my own breath. Smoke pouring

from my mouth in the cold. Memory, interloper in the corner who means to kill,

heavy rock in its hand. And poetry. This poem right now. This one-night stand.

Those days, if I consider them disjointed from what came later,

like horsetail reeds, they're profuse in this part of the world, or were,

you can pull them apart in segments and put them back together again,

those days of fishing for rock bass in a boat with a slow leak and no motor,

the pond so clear we could see the star grass and clasping-leaf on the gold

bottom, son still a kid and fairly OK, not as happy as some kids but happy

enough, and we were happy enough, I don't believe in true love, marriage

is a negotiation we were ill-equipped to navigate, we thought having noble

ideals was sufficient, married for 100 bucks and that included yellow

cake and Xeroxed invitations with quotes from early suffragettes, I married

him because he painted *Rolling Stones* in the bell tower of the church where

he was forced to usher as a kid, told myself a story about what that meant

about him and hence what it meant about me, so not *those were the days*,

just those days, not so bad if unhooked from their affiliated calamities.

The world today is wet, the world is wet, trees

not so much dripping as exuding, walnuts dropping,

bouncing off the roof, sound of 100 small skulls

thwacked with a bat, releasing their green,

luscious acridity, then stillness, which Lorca called

an apprenticeship to death, long blue wind chimes

stopped in their tracks, who in their right mind would

entrust music to the wind, love stops, let's not say

otherwise, out of the blue it arrives chuffing black

smoke then departs with a scream like Spanish trains

in the '70s, jump on, eat a bocadillo, blow a wet harmonica

with a guitarist you'll never see again who plays Dylan's

version of "Baby Please Don't Go," now thunder, now

a cloudburst, now a weird, bending spectrum in the sky.

The small stuff, the care and feeding of things, chameleons.

I choose melons well and adequate to the job of reviving

the dead, I've done it, officially, three times. Nails: their pounding.

I remember a time I was bad at everything but rhyme, the teacher

slapped me for peeing myself, she had breast cancer so all is forgiven,

such as when she forced kids to eat the things they hated in hot

lunch until they heaved. I couldn't stand it when she read to us,

the slow gears of her voice. On the playground, I hallucinated

the devil, small and potent as that place between my legs, opened

the drawstring of the cloth bag and spilled out my marbles, held

each up to the sun and one in my mouth to taste its coolness,

how expertly I now work a twist tie around the mouth of a bag,

socks, keep them in pairs, dole out thin slices of apple

on the rocks near the big lake in the fog, here, take and eat.

I can't see her clearly. Can you see your mother clearly? I was concocted

in the kettle of her body. Swam like a swan in a pool of her blood. From my

earliest days I called her by her name. But inside, always mommy. I called

out to her, even when I was far from home. In High Wycombe, peeling

peaches for dinner. Not like that, a stern woman said, telling me to slip the knife

just under the skin and pull it away from the flesh. Peeing outside the Hellfire

Caves on Midsummer Night. In Scotland, sleeping in a tent on the cold ground.

So far north the sky never got dark. Arrested in Germany for stealing a mug.

Man wearing lederhosen barking at me. Veins in his face ready to explode. Forced

to eat that awful white sausage the color of an underbelly. Bad strawberries. Shitting

myself on the train from Segovia. Giving birth, cut through the gut, the layer of fat

and uterus exposed to the cold room and its attendants. And now in my solitude

which matches her solitude like mother-daughter dresses she'd disdain. Do you see

how I persist in telling you about the flowers when I mean to describe the rain?

It won't kill me to be sad again for just a little while, it was a sad day

though not a tragic day, a stranger yelled at me, a real solid drive-by,

hatred in his eyes, my neighbor said he could have had a gun and I

shouldn't have back-talked, but I just can't be spoken to that way anymore

even if in the end whoever-it-is grabs their whatever and blows a hole

clean through some part of me, and it was sad seeing mom again, nothing

bad happened, just meeting up with her in that hole-in-the-wall on Red

Arrow Highway with the half-ass tacos, it's a clean place, the people are

nice, what's to be sad about except for the taxidermized brown bear

in the entryway and us not getting any younger, driving home, lunch was

too short, it's always too short, we have to steel ourselves for these farewells,

in the fields the corn was pretty much played out, the grapes this year not

so great, the vines my son planted didn't produce, taking a break maybe

or done for good, there is such a thing, you know, as done for good.

I wish I still smoked so that I could sit outside in the dark

and smoke rather than just sitting outside in the dark. I'm glad

my parents smoked even if it gave me asthma. It was worth it

to hear the roar of the match and watch them bring fire so close

to their faces and from across the room or yard to see the lit end

grow angry and then out of their mouths came a smoke dragon

that climbed and swelled in the air. I'm about to be poor. I'll live

as my mother has lived. Dish soap and dryer sheets and birdseed

and greeting cards from the dollar store. Yet not being a tightwad.

She's like Jesus with the loaves and fishes, always a few bucks to slip

into somebody's hand but never the collection plate. Unlike Shirl

who held so long to a penny that it turned green in her hand. In this

way, I don't need a Bible. The parables are there like the free cigarettes

tobacco companies handed out to patients in mental institutions.

The sonnet, like poverty, teaches you what you can do
without. To have, as my mother says, a wish in one hand
and shit in another. That was in answer to I wish I had
an Instamatic camera and a father. Wish in one hand, she
said, shit in another. She still says it. When she tells me
she wishes I were there to have some of her bean soup
she answers herself. Wish in one hand, she says, shit in another.
Poverty, like a sonnet, is a good teacher. The kind that raps your
knuckles with a ruler but not the kind that throws a dictionary
across the room and hits you in the brain with all the words
that ever were. Boxed fathers buried deep are still fathers,
teacher says. Do without *the*. Without *and*. Without hot
dogs in your baked beans. A sonnet is a mother. Every word
a silver dollar. Shit in one hand, she says. Wish in another.

My favorite scent is my own funk, my least favorite scent, other

people's funk, and this, my friends, is why we cannot have nice

things. I value the advice I give others but I don't like the advice

that comes my way unless it reflects what I would have done anyway.

You know how it goes. I like how my voice sounds in the car

when I sing along with Earth, Wind & Fire but no one else can

pull it off, no one. My bad acting, when I acted, was charming.

I intended it to be bad, as a comment on the state of theater

in the 20th century. On days I don't have to see anyone I don't brush

my hair, I don't wear underwear or shoes or chemical potions meant

to extinguish my funk, and in these times, I am nearly perfectly happy.

If you're me, it's luxurious to go unobserved. When asked the inevitable

question, whether I'd wear eyeliner if I was the last person on earth,

no, hell no. Eyeliner is war. When I'm alone, I lay my weapons down.

You know what living means? Tits out, tits in the rain. Tits

in the cereal bowl. Tits ablaze. What beauty there was is now

on the wane. I've seen beauty tinkle in the spring its little

breeze-borne bells. Summer's copper gong, heat frizzing

the wisteria until all that's left is rat hair. Winter, I think

there are ice flutes. I think blue lips of killed kids blow cold

notes from ice flutes. You know what living's for? Tits

sacrosanct. Declined. Tits blued by cold, insomnia, midnight,

indigoed like collapsed veins, steel-blue-stained pillowcase

of the crone whose nightie won't be pulled up anymore.

I saw my tits when I was young reflected back to me in a blue

mirror on which were laid out lines of coke. Even then

they were old, savant-tits, they knew things. Purpled.

Milked-out. Mounded low and moving slow in the old way.

Marry dull. Those who retain full access to their imaginations are crosshatched bitches. They may look good from a certain angle, wearing a tight black slip as a skin with their furry legs dangling out the bottom and cornflower boots that originated at some defunct box store and were donated with the soles worn thin and then stolen—*stolen*—from a St. Vincent de Paul while a defrocked nun had her back turned fumigating bras for resale. Don't marry that. Its boots all jingle-jangle. It's not going to loan out its rain hat. Or adopt a calf. I learned to read at age three. Used a toilet plunger to suck ants out of their holes. One doll danced, another spoke in tongues. What do you want from me? If you rotate me like a jewel you will locate the flaw that runs all the way through like a pulsing vein of gold that brings in the fat-cat colonizers who ruin everything that came before. The fish. The birds. The actual human people. Don't marry that. Go for something with half of an imagination. Half or a fourth. Like Mikel instructed about his ashes: A fourth to his mother. A fourth to me. I disobeyed, slit the phony box and set all of him free.

Lately I've been feeling about poetry like sex. Now and then I'm in

the mood but then the mood doesn't bloom. The thought of it makes me

a little sick to my stomach. Lead-up, lead-in, cleanup. Mixing of martini,

metaphor, or the hard bangery of no metaphor at all. Cumbersome *I* like

a big dick you have to handle. The *we* with all that *we are getting ice cream, we*

are thinking about getting a cat. How does *we* think about stuff? Is it a brain stem

thing? An art I never mastered. I have met people who would bang Ted

Hughes on Plath's grave and then write about it. *I, too, bit his cheek.* That

sort of crap. Yeah, I, too, have been that person. I want to say *at times.*

Long ago. I'm better now. Really I'm just tireder. A guy, I'm going to name him

Delaney, once said to me when I wanted to be done with him, *now that you've had*

your little orgasm, murder in his eyes. I called down all the angels from the skies

to get him out the door so I could bolt it and wash him off of me. His big

hand reaching for my throat. The prayer I prayed. That was sex and poetry.

Ever since Elise brought up that Marianne Moore poem, "No Swan

so Fine," published in *Poetry* in 1932 which is a long time ago, well it was

Johannes who exposed her to the poem, or the poem to her, and then

she exposed it to me, you know how poetry operates, like syphilis, which is

on the rise, well ever since Elise brought up "No Swan so Fine," a really

majestic poem, and strange, I said it's like a poem by a femme Wallace Stevens,

and now I think it's like Stevens being placed in a corset against his will,

and sticks out his lower lip like a baby but grows to like the concision,

the visceral feeling of restraint, ever since "No Swan so Fine," which was only

a few hours ago, I can't stop thinking that Marianne Moore was born in or near

St. Louis, Missouri, and I will be there soon, my dog and me, my rental will have

three bedrooms, I wonder what I'll do with the 2 and ¾ extra bedrooms as I will

occupy only ¼ of the one I choose to call mine, I sleep very little, and when I do

I am as still as that photograph of Marianne Moore, old, wearing a tri-corner hat.

My private parts are many, my teeth are private, my tongue, the buoy

of my brain bobbing in its cloistered sea, my eye's vitreous detachment,

the lightning that crackled when the membrane broke inside my eye, I

was at a Kmart roving among female sanitary products, each in its private

firing chamber, and a flock of crows rose in my vision and never since

has found a branch to land on, the flock's voice private, my own voice box's

wet surreptitious lid opens to the jewelry-box ballerina who keeps my tune

whirling, and what is beneath her gauze skirt is private, and the hole in the crotch

of my pants, and my memory of the bloodstain on the crotch of the yoga

teacher's sleek leggings private, my viscera, as if some scalpel could penetrate

me, some X-ray could make my fractures glow, my first love was not a football

player who wiped my tears with his dirty sock, who grew into a fireman

and fell through the roof, my first love was a phallus of cheap perfume,

a small black bottle from the mall, a clandestine phallus called femme fatale.

Back then its hair was Cleopatraed but went toward witch, back then when

it was office chick it would prop its leg on a wooden desk while smoking cigs

and typing memos for professors who pulled their beards and asked if they

could bum a ciggie it had a pleasing plumpness, it lined its eyes, its hair was

henna-blue a kind of heron-blue, its plumpness pleasing then, a bit unkempt

a little soft but it got out of hand and went all the way to big and then to large

and then to grand, pregnancy and psychotropic meds, food will do that to a body,

it walks down the avenue like Queen Lou fingers green under worthless rings,

hair escaping pins, then it had a baby voice, even its sex voice was tinged

with embryo, now it sounds like a bad crash, car driven too fast around a bow

in the road, windows unrolled, kid dead in his cock-surety upside down in the wreck

on the swamp edge before the cops arrive, ungreased wheels still spinning, singing

out their rust and on the radio "Summertime" sung as sex and death rattle, its voice

like baby teeth in a dryer drum, a bitch's diary on fire and only frogs to overhear.

To say that I'm a witch makes me feel better all-round,

lets me off a kind of hook, not fishhook, meat hook, despair,

the green cast of my hair, the bitter greens I grow and cook

and consume in inopportune mouthfuls, mouthfuls by which

I consumed, in the past, my life. Did I consume my life in bitter

mouthfuls? The storytelling makes it seem so but in actuality

I dragged a bit my heels, preserving myself like a bloody

rhubarb compote in a crock for something later, better, bitterer,

and here I am in the ever-later looking back at the half-assery

of my days and the redness of my nights, innard-red, preserved

in my skull like intestines in a Canopic jar, God, the vinegar,

the brine, the pseudo-deliciousness of my time, and was I always

better at eating it than growing it, casting spells than spelling it,

depicting a witch than witching it, telling it than living it?

After forty years of forced estrangement soul mate shows up

in the lobby of a gold hotel she's haggard with a loose cough her

eyes disappear into her skull if she doesn't wear eyeliner we used

to dress as Daryl Hall and John Oates and make brief appearances

at parties or Bowie and Liz Taylor she had a terrible dog named

Wanda who ate Galway Kinnell's signature off *The Book of Nightmares*

I mean Galway Kinnell signed it for me he wrote for Diane and her

poems or some such flummery Etheridge Knight wrote for Sister

Diane and her poems now that has some meat that has some sugar

soul mate's hair is pink her talons sharp she has received as have I

the blessing of an extinguished sex drive listen she says after forty

goddamned years of forced estrangement guess who I saw in Malibu

he's famous and he has a huge head and I say without even

having to think about it Tom Waits and soul mate says Bingo.

For me it's going be to something simple, like Kylie Jenner dressing daughter

Stormi as Kylie Jenner for Halloween. Or hearing some woman described

as having had a bubbly personality, as if that should have staved off murder.

I'd move to Iceland, but Iceland won't have me. Anywhere really with emptiness

and socialized medicine. All I ask for is a hut with a moss roof but how many

sufferers on this planet have a whole hut to themselves with a moss roof.

There are some hard things coming up. You know what they are. We all face them,

though if you're rich it's a little easier I hear, independent living, assisted living,

memory care, skilled nursing muffling the path to the crematory. Damon, raised

in Flint, his co-op job was working for a cemetery, he was the guy who waved

a big magnet over the ashes to pull out the metal, told me what ends up in the urn

is a conglomeration of you and everybody ever born. It's like an airplane

with no first class. That democracy of death thing. From Damon I learned

a lot but not what happens to a body without the money to be burned.

I courted her, that musky tart, dusk personified, she of the purple prose and yellow

journalism, her claws the color of Gaugin's Christ, pee-pee yellow with a dash of green,

like that algae called xantho-something-or-other, missing its fucoxanthin, thus yellow-green,

like poor-people teeth, like the finger and toenails of boozehounds, come to me, I said,

her mouth like day two of a bad period, can hardly get up from her stool without that wooden

cane with a stiletto in the tip of the shaft in case somebody gets local, but to quote my cousin-

who-looks-like-Moses speaking of Etta James, "she's old, she's fat, she's sick, she's mean,

she's the sexiest thing I've ever seen," like this girl who showed up at my door, she knocked

and I answered and she just stood there in her tatters staring at me and picking her nose,

sized me up like I should be the one ashamed of myself, she had a point to make, I guess,

something about the grotesque, and Caren whose head was too small for her body who later

became a cop and then a minister, said that I embodied that song "Femme Fatale" by the Velvet

Underground, "false-colored eyes" and all, well now I'm barely femme and fatal only to some,

my kidney hurts, I debrided my own burn, that loneliness I once lusted for I have become.

My tits are bruised as if I've been with a rough lover but I have

not been, not today, I once gentled a certain someone and it turns

out I loathe gentle, and bought a hard, red pear, hard enough

to pound a nail into a reenactment crucifix, and I left the hard pear,

I mean dick-hard, on the red windowsill, abandoned it to its solo

ripening until it began to exude that familiar musk, it might as well

have said eat me, or sung it soprano, but the more it wanted my

teeth in its hide the more I dodged it, I'd lost all respect for it,

like that poem in which ripening plums are evidence that eternity

is illogical, well of course it's illogical, and by the time I decided

to just go ahead and dive, it had broken out with a bad case of fruit

flies, my fault indeed but I blamed the pear, let's all blame the pear,

this is not a metaphor but a fable whose moral is as old as time:

I'm worried about these bruises and who will hold me when I die?

I hope when it happens I have time to say oh so this is how it is happening

unlike Frank hit by a jeep on Fire Island but not like dad who knew too

long six goddamn years in a young man's life so long it made a sweet guy sarcastic

I want enough time to say oh so this is how I'll go and smirk at that last rhyme

I rhymed at times because I wanted to make something pretty especially for Mikel

who liked pretty things soft and small things who cried into a white towel when I hurt

myself when it happens I don't want to be afraid I want to be curious was Mikel curious

I'm afraid by then he was only sad he had no money left was living on green oranges

had kissed all his friends goodbye I kissed lips that kissed Frank's lips though not

for me a willing kiss I willingly kissed lips that kissed Howard's deathbed lips

I happily kissed lips that kissed lips that kissed Basquiat's lips I know a man who said

he kissed lips that kissed lips that kissed lips that kissed lips that kissed Whitman's

lips who will say of me I kissed her who will say of me I kissed someone who kissed

her or I kissed someone who kissed someone who kissed someone who kissed her.

Notes

The cover photograph is of Mikel Lindzy, a central figure in the book, taken by his friend and lover Alan Martinez in the early 1980s. Alan writes: "I'm unsure, but I think we were in LA horsing around in a cheap motel room off of Cahuenga Blvd. It's hard to remember, but it had to be the trip where we went down to Tijuana to get some stuff that was rumored to be an HIV drug. We also went to Disneyland, of which I have no memories, and Zuma Beach, near Malibu. The ocean, of course, made Mikel nervous. Our friend Joe remembers the trip in the photo differently. He said it was probably after a bunch of us went down to my hometown to experience the Santa Maria Elks Rodeo and Parade. So that would make the photo maybe from '81, '82, just before AIDS. But I do remember taking the picture. We were just kind of clowning around and he struck a pose to be goofy. You can see he's mocking the pose as he's doing it. I think you're the only person in the world he would have let use the photo. I think he would say, 'well, if she wants it, she can use it.'"

The epigraph by Candy Darling is from her book, *Candy Darling: Memoirs of an Andy Warhol Superstar*.

The epigraph "Feel like a lady, and you my lady boy" is from Amy Winehouse's song "Stronger Than Me" on her first album, *Frank*.

The epigraph quoting Elaine de Kooning is from *Word of Mouth: Gossip and American Poetry*, by Chad Bennett.

"[What is it you feel I asked Kurt]," "[Listening to 'Summertime']," and "[There is a certain state of grace]" emerged from conversations and correspondence with musician and composer Kurt Rohde. The last two lines in "[I should have been in cinema]" also came from a conversation with Kurt and student musicians at the University of California in Davis.

The quotation in "[My first night in New York]" is from *A Lover's Discourse: Fragments* by Roland Barthes.

"[Freelance artist. That's what you say]" was written by Dylan Seuss-Brakeman and is published here with his permission.

The poems on pages 71–77 are from conversations with my son Dylan. Many of the lines are his, verbatim, and are used with his permission.

The lyrics in "[Then when I grew up]" are from "Willin'," a song written by Lowell George and performed by Little Feat on their first studio album, *Little Feat*. The invented lyrics in the same poem are by Dylan Seuss-Brakeman.

The phrase "The charismatic impresario of all we did" in "[He said it bummed him out his dick]" and "Through all these myriad felt and mostly scorned and disreputable realities" in "[Death does not exist in poetry]" are both from unpublished poems by Alan Martinez and used with his permission.

Keats's description of Fanny Brawne, "—her Arms are good, her hands bad-ish," in "[Abrupt lines on the nature of beauty]" is from a letter to his brother George, dated December 16, 1818.

In "[My literary tastes of late are manic]," the lines "the wife of the engineer Gliebov, who has been killed hunting, was there. She sang a great deal," are from *Note-Book of Anton Chekhov*, translated by S. S. Koteliansky and Leonard Woolf.

"Dick's," mentioned in "[And then landscape was all there was]," is in Las Vegas, New Mexico.

"[Takes time to get to minimalism]" mentions ideas gleaned from reading Gregory Orr's essay "The Two Survivals" in his book *Poetry as Survival*.

Acknowledgments

The Academy of American Poets' *Poem-a-Day*—"[What is it you feel I asked Kurt]," "[There is a force that breaks the body]," "[Things feel partial. My love for things is partial]."

The Account—"[Mountains black today, hiding]," "[Either all of this is an apparition or I am]," "[For twenty-six days I lived]," "[It is abominable, unquenchable by touch]," "[And then landscape was all there was]."

The Adroit Journal—"[I should have been in cinema]," "[Parties among strangers]."

The American Poetry Review—"[My earliest memory]," "[Labels now slip off me like clothes]," "[Abrupt lines on the nature of beauty]," "[We all have our trauma nadir]," [Goldenrod, I could say, you know]," [I hope when it happens]."

BOATT—"[Maybe we wander]."

Brevity—"[I hoisted them, two drug dealers]."

BuzzFeed—"[The famous poets came for us]."

Court Green—"[My first night in New York]," "[My tits are bruised]," "[I dreamed a color, no plot, a color]," "[I could do it. I could walk into the sea]" "[I want drugs again; whimsy]," "[I want to zero in on what he looked like]," "[He said it bummed him out his dick]," "[Death does not exist in poetry]," "[I saw a little movie of a person stroking]," "[The sonnet, like poverty]."

Crazyhorse—"[The White Rabbit was before]," "[The fat suffering of the farrowing sow]," "[The patriarch of Jesus Camp is dead]."

G U E S T: A Journal of Guest Editors—"[Thirty-nine years ago is nothing]," "[Lately I've been feeling about poetry]."

Guesthouse—"[I'm watching *A Face in the Crowd*]," "[I can't rest, can't get no relief]."

Gulf Coast—"[How do you stand being so virtuous]," "[OD'd on his Suboxone]," "[Marry dull]," "[You know what living means]," "[Back then its hair was Cleopatraed]," "[He called from San Francisco]."

The Kenyon Review—"[I drove all the way to Cape Disappointment]," "['No need to sparkle']," "[I aborted two daughters]," "[To return from Paradise]," "[The best is when you respond]," "[Poetry, the only father, landscape]," "[I've lived with death from the beginning]," "[From this bench I like to call my bench]."

The Missouri Review—"[Takes time to get to minimalism]," "[Once, I took a Greyhound north]," "[My first crush was Wild Bill Hickok]," "[His body was barely cold]," "[I can't see her clearly]," "[I can't say I loved punk]," "[What do you think Elvis's best song was]," "[Then, I account it high time to get to sea]."

The New Yorker—"[I have slept in many places]."

On the Seawall—"[I dreamed I had to find my way]," "[There is a certain state of grace]," "[My literary tastes of late are manic]."

Ploughshares—"[To say that I'm a witch]," "[All lives have their tropes]," "[The problem with sweetness is death]."

Plume—"[Intimacy unhinged, unpaddocked me]," "[I met a man a dying man]," "[It's that time of spring]," "[The emergent self is not a self that loves]," "[The world today is wet]," "[Freak accidents do happen]," "[The small stuff, the care]," "[I suck so many cough drops]," "[All things now remind me]."

Quarterly West—"[For a couple years, I slept nights]," "[I was not a large child]," "[I've encountered the exoskeleton]."

The Rumpus—"[He came to us all the way down here with us]," "[That bar, World of the Satisfyin' Place]," "[My private parts are many]," "[My favorite scent is my own funk]."

Scoundrel Time—"[I wish I still smoked]," "[Yes, I saw them all, saw them, met some]," "[Margaret Sanger did the first one]."

Shenandoah—"[To say that I'm a witch]," "[All lives have their tropes]," "[The problem with sweetness is death]."

Sporklet—"[For me it's going to be]," "[Literature is dangerous business]."

Virginia Quarterly Review—"[After the pigs and lambs and rabbits]," "[I dreamed of it again, my dad's body]," "[The lambs this year are dumb]," "[Where is the drug to drug]," "[I fell on an incline, talus, tibia]."

Waxwing Literary Journal—"[Here on this edge]," "[Sometimes I can't feel it]," "[Press a foot into this beach]," "[I courted her, that musky tart]," "[How will I leave this life, like I left my job]," "[On what day do you think Jesus]," "[I floated I flew I fell to Earth]."

West Branch—"[There's something to be said for having]," "[All at once David went catatonic]," "[After forty years]."

My deepest gratitude to:

Willapa Bay AIR for time, space, collaboration, and community.

Thank you to Graywolf Press: Director and Publisher Fiona McCrae, Executive Editor Jeff Shotts, Editorial and Production Associate Chantz Erolin, and the entire staff.

Friends and Confidants: Aaron Coleman, Kelly Cressio-Moeller, Justin Danzy, Patrick Donnelly, Gail Griffin, Liz Henderson, Conrad Hilberry, Jane Hilberry, Elise Houcek, Jane Huffman, Karen Kornblum, Tara Labovich, Daniel Menzo, Gabe Montesanti, Pam Poley, Dave Posther, Aaron Smith, and Gail Wronsky.

My family: Deb Dew, my sister, her husband, Dewey, nieces Rachel, Emily, and Katie; Dylan, my son; my mother and father, Norma and Robert Seuss.

Special appreciation and love to collaborators Alan Martinez, Kurt Rohde, and Dylan Seuss-Brakeman.

And Mikel Lindzy—"I wouldn't want to be faster / or greener than now if you were with me O you / were the best of all my days"—Frank O'Hara, "Animals."

Diane Seuss is the author of five poetry collections, including *frank: sonnets*, winner of the Pulitzer Prize, the National Book Critics Circle Award, the Los Angeles Times Book Prize, and the PEN/Voelcker Award for Poetry Collection; *Still Life with Two Dead Peacocks and a Girl*, a finalist for the National Book Critics Circle Award and the Los Angeles Times Book Prize; and *Four-Legged Girl*, a finalist for the Pulitzer Prize. In 2020 she received a Guggenheim Fellowship, and in 2021 she received the John Updike Award from the American Academy of Arts and Letters. She lives in rural Michigan.

The text of *frank: sonnets* is set in Adobe Garamond Pro.

Book design by Rachel Holscher.

Composition by Bookmobile Design and Digital Publisher Services, Minneapolis, Minnesota.

Manufactured by Versa Press on acid-free, 30 percent postconsumer wastepaper.